Why was this gift given us and what are we to do with it?

ALEKSANDR I. SOLZHENITSYN
1970 NOBEL PRIZE LECTURE

LORD, shall we not bring these gifts to Your service?

T. S. ELIOT
CHORUSES FROM THE ROCK

THE
LIBERATING
WORD: *Art and the Mystery of the Gospel*

by D. Bruce Lockerbie

WILLIAM B. EERDMANS
PUBLISHING COMPANY   Grand Rapids

for Lory

Library of Congress Cataloging in Publication Data

Lockerbie, D Bruce.
The liberating word.

Includes bibliographical references.
1. Creation.   2. Creation (Literary, artistic, etc.).
3. Christian literature — History and criticism.
I.   Title.
BS652.L6   218   74-8928
ISBN 0-8028-1586-3

contents

acknowledgments

Some of the early drafts of this book were delivered as lectures at The Stony Brook School, Stony Brook, New York; at the University of Mississippi, Oxford, Mississippi; and to meetings of the New Jersey Association of Teachers of English and the New England Association of Teachers of Christian Schools. To these several audiences my thanks for serving as early sounding boards.

Parts of the book have also appeared as essays in *Eternity* and *Christianity Today*, although in somewhat different form.

Excerpts from the poetry of T. S. Eliot are reprinted from his volume, *Collected Poems* 1909-1962, by permission of Harcourt Brace Jovanovich, Inc.; copyright, 1936, by Harcourt Brace Jovanovich, Inc.;̇ copyright © 1963, 1964, by T. S. Eliot. Also reprinted by permission of Faber and Faber Ltd. from *Collected Poems* 1909-1962.

Excerpts from *The Honorary Consul* by Graham Greene are reprinted by permission of Simon and Schuster, Inc. Copyright © 1973 by Graham Greene.

Most biblical quotations are from *The New English Bible*. Copyright © The Delegates of the Oxford University Press and the Syndics of the Cambridge University Press 1961, 1970. Reprinted by permission.

preface

For some time I've been thinking about what we casually call "creativity" and where it comes from. What makes one man a painter and another a house painter? What drives one person to write poetry while another contents himself with sloganeering on Madison Avenue? Why is one man holding an acetylene torch a sculptor and another a steelworker?

Given my beliefs in Creation and the nature of the Creator, I thought a good place to begin looking for an answer to these questions would be the Bible. From this primary text, I moved on to various books on aesthetics, poetics, and myth. In the summer of 1972, I read a curious essay by B. F. Skinner, in which he both posed the question and implied an answer: "Does the poet create, originate, initiate the thing called a poem, or is his behavior merely the product of his genetic and environmental histories?" For Skinner the implied answer is that "having a poem is like having a baby." Just as the mother is merely "a locus" where something biological happens, so the poet is also "a place in which certain genetic and environmental causes come together to have a common effect." Such reasoning follows conveniently, of course, from premises laid down in books such as *Beyond Freedom and Dignity*. For the author who can say in all seriousness, "To man *qua* man we say good riddance," it's perfectly reasonable to conclude that the poet's only source for his art may be found in his genes and environment.

It's also reasonable for Skinner and his followers to ridicule belief in either "a creative Mind" (his phrase) or a personal God. Skinner must consider either concept as little more than an outmoded appeal to primitive authority. He's puzzled that sophisticated modern man, who has abandoned (so Skinner asserts) his traditional belief in a creative Mind "with respect to the creation of the world," should nonetheless "fight so desperately to preserve it in respect to the creation of a poem."

Because I'm a Christian, I believe the Bible helps to explain Skinner's conundrum. There is, I'm sure, an inherent relationship between God's act of Creation and man's desire to make something that expresses his uniqueness in the order of that Creation. In this little book, I'm interested in looking at this relationship. But beyond that, I'm also interested in seeing the uses to which man puts his imagination, committed in service to his Creator.

Because I'm a Christian, I also believe that it's providential that, after I was well into writing the final draft of this book, I came upon a 1950 essay by Denis de Rougemont, "Religion and the Mission of the Artist," in which I found this statement: "Thus, to meditate upon the mystery of the Father, would be to lead at one and the same time to the best understanding of the act of the artist, and to its limits or its relativity."

I'm sure I have more in common with de Rougemont than with Skinner.

—D. B. L.
Stony Brook, N. Y.

THE
LIBERATING
WORD

CHAPTER ONE

the poet is being used

The aroma of freshly baked bread calls up in me some of the most pleasurable recollections from my childhood. For a time when I was a little boy, my father was a bread salesman. He often took me with him to the bakery, where I saw the hundreds of loaves being removed from the ovens, where I helped stock the horse-drawn wagon. The fact that I sometimes was allowed to hold the horse's reins along the delivery route may also be a factor in my memory. But I'm not particularly fond of horses; it's fresh baked bread and that warm, intoxicating fragrance of yeast and dough becoming crust that appeal to me. At home I regarded my mother's baking bread to be as good as a feast, with butter and jam melting into the moist texture. My wife still knows and sometimes gratifies my taste for homemade bread.

In a different way something in me stirs whenever I sense the combination of smells from a railroad train. I was born in one of Canada's principal railroad junction towns. There the Canadian National's eastbound trains from Winnipeg and westbound from Toronto met and turned around. I was very young when my parents left the Northern Ontario village; I have returned only twice in my life. But wherever I have gone, the odors of steam and burning cinder linger, even in these decadent days of diesel and electrification. To me one of man's most civilizing experiences is to ride a luxury train — alas, an ever diminishing possibility today. I know what Emily Dickinson meant when she wrote,

> I like to see it lap the Miles,
> And lick the Valleys up.

Why should these two scents remain lodged so in my consciousness? Is my delight in the smell of baking bread a psycho-

13

logical yearning for the assurance of the hearth, a mythic influence? Is my fascination with locomotives a search for power, an assertion of my masculinity, a return of that mythic wanderlust inhabiting the spirits of all men? Perhaps so. All I know is that they are part of my imagination, memory, dreams, and always in pleasing associations.

Conversely the sense of smell can also remind me of a most unpleasant experience. Whenever I sniff the scent of ether or an antiseptic, I remember my fright at being taken, as a boy of six, to the local armory in my Canadian city to receive mandatory innoculations against diphtheria and scarlet fever. Hundreds of children stood in long lines with their parents. As the lines progressed toward their terminal points somewhere in the armory, one could catch the scent of solutions being applied to each arm simultaneously by nurses. Almost uniformly, it seemed to me, with the first touch of the cold liquid to the skin, the child began to cry. His crying increased to protestations against taking one more step, for ahead on each side loomed the syringe-wielding doctors themselves. But there was no turning back. If the parents were unable to constrain the child forward, a Canadian soldier—his Montgomery beret and plaid puttees stand out in my memory—was ready to end the foolishness and move the child along.

To this day, I can recall my father's icy control of voice when he said (as much for my benefit as for the soldier's), "It won't be necessary to help this fellow, thank you." I never even felt the injections! My next clear memory is of standing outside the armory eating a promised ice-cream cone, earned by my demonstration of courage.

The smell of medicinal solutions, I say, is responsible for evoking in me this recollection; however, even ice cream can sometimes start the process of association that leads me back to the same event. Any of several words, whatever the context in which they appear, can also call up this incident in my memory: *antiseptic, ether, inoculation, syringe*—I'm afraid of them all. But none of these words and not even the smells themselves can diagram fully the experience as I remember it or as my consciousness knows it.

Imagination, memory, dreams—the reservoir of our deepest longings, the vault in which we store and from which we draw spontaneously our recollections of sorrow or joy, fright or pleasure. Who understands them? Who can explain the phenomenon of *déjà vu*, that eerie sense of having experienced before a place or event we can't be sure we have ever actually experienced? How little it takes to excite a response from the imagination! How retentive and categorical the memory can be of details forgotten to consciousness! How uncontrollable our dreams, our fantasies!

Imagination, memory, and dreams are more than passive storage areas within us. They are also active forces working upon our consciousness through which we receive the stimulus for art. Of course, some scientists would disagree. The purely mechanistic behaviorist sees the brain as an organ responsive to electrical impulses, not unlike the computers in his lab. What the brain produces, according to his view, is the direct result of measurable inputs. The biochemist may have another explanation. He may look for stimuli from the body's nervous system, circulatory system, digestive system. Depending entirely on how the artist "feels," his product will be bright and splashy or sombre and brooding. This explanation is not unrelated to the ancient notion of the four "humors" of the body. Physiologists through the Middle Ages and long after believed a man to be controlled by his dominating bodily fluids—phlegm, blood, yellow bile, or black bile. A man's temperament was described as phlegmatic, sanguine, choleric, or melancholic, according to whichever "humor" was supposed to dominate him.

Does art depend upon the cells and acids within the artist? Perhaps, but the poet Stanley Burnshaw has another suggestion. In a remarkable book called *The Seamless Web*, he writes,

> Like anyone else, a creative artist inhales the surrounding world and exhales it. Whatever is taken in is given back in altered condition or transformed into matter, action, feeling, thought. And in the case of creative persons, an additional exhalation: in the form or words or sounds or shapes capable of acting upon others with the force of an object alive in their surrounding worlds.

Another word for *inhales* is, of course, *inspires*. The artist breathes in the surrounding world; it is his inspiration. His art is his expiration.

But even this explanation is inadequate, for we must go back to ask questions about the origins of both the artist himself and his surrounding world. Where did they come from? Who placed the artist in his inspirational environment? By what processes does the artist give back his inspiration "in altered condition or transformed into matter, action, feeling, thought"? What is the wellspring, the source, that fills the reservoir? Where do imagination, memory, and dreams come from?

Brewster Ghiselin speaks of the artist's receiving

> a vague, even a confused excitement, some sort of yearning, hunch, or other preverbal intimation of approaching or potential resolution. Stephen Spender's expression is exact: "a dim cloud of an idea which I feel must be condensed into a shower of words." Alfred North Whitehead speaks of "the state of imaginative muddled suspense which precedes successful inductive generalization," and there is much other testimony to the same effect.

Burnshaw sums up his effort to locate the source for artistic inspiration, saying, "The act of composition remains as surprising as ever to the poet, who knows only one thing for certain: that he is *being used*."

Being used by whom and to what end? we may ask. One question leads to another, but are there no answers? Psychologists from Sigmund Freud to the present agree, in principle, that the miracle of art and the source of its inspiration baffle them beyond all ability to explain. The simplest formula seems to be that the human being receives his inspiration from somewhere— I intend to argue that God is that source. The artist perceives sights, sounds, or other appeals to his senses. He receives visions, revelations, epiphanies. All compel him to respond. He feels obliged to explore those dim intimations, perhaps to identify on canvas or on a keyboard or on paper what he has seen or heard in his mind. He struggles, then, to give shape to that urge within him, to search out the meanings of his quest, to find its purposes; to work from amorphousness to form and there— if he is fortunate—to learn a paradoxical truth about art suggested by C. S. Lewis, "You find out what the moral is by writing the story." Lewis means that the artist himself may have no more concrete idea of what his finished work is to be than does the reader opening the first page of a novel or a listener settling down to hear an unfamiliar piece of music. The artist, like his audience, engages in the act of *discovery*.

Often the artist is frustrated and disappointed by the results of his endeavor to objectify his artistic vision. Let me offer another childhood reminiscence. I dreaded art class throughout elementary school. I must have lacked the essential electrical impulses or biochemical juices that might have equipped me for the formal study of art. I was never able to sketch or paint a picture that suggested even the slightest measure of ability. To my astonishment other boys and girls could produce the most delightful crayon pictures of flowers, birds, sunsets, and all. My work looked like angry smudges on grocery bags. Yet when I spoke approvingly of my classmates' work, or when the teacher came around the desks and commended these gifted children, they always said the same thing. They always said, "Oh, it didn't turn out."

Of course it didn't *turn out!* It couldn't turn out! It never will turn out, if by that remark one means, "I did not adequately convey in colored wax or in Carrara marble or in polyphonic harmony or in iambic pentameter the greater vision that is stored within me." Why must this be so? Why does Igor Stravinsky despair after conducting a performance of his work, "It is never good enough, never!" Why does the poet Edna St. Vincent Millay write to her publisher, "Many of my poems, of course, are greatly reduced in stature from the majesty which I had hoped they might achieve, because I was unable, as one often is, to make the poem rise up to my conception of it"? Because any painter, sculptor, musician, poet soon comes to recognize his fundamental dilemma: How to reconcile the contrast between the grandeur of his inspiration and the failure of his expression?

To my recollection none of my art teachers in school ever consoled those children whose work didn't turn out by instructing them in this first principle of aesthetics. But neither did they go on to tell these frustrated pupils *why* their efforts failed to satisfy, why every artist worthy of the name feels the same dissatisfaction, even when he has exceeded any other man's accomplishment.

Some time ago I listened to a broadcast recording of an unusual musical composition, the tone poem by Allan Hovhaness called "And God Created Great Whales." This work is for symphony orchestra and the recorded sounds of whales, a powerfully affecting work. Hovhaness has taken the natural sounds of whales and blended with them the sounds from within his own imagination—perhaps also taken from memory or dreams. He has expressed these sounds in a language familiar to musicians: notations on musical staves, lines and curlicues and numbers, a patchwork blueprint with instructions in Italian. The New York Philharmonic and the conductor who commissioned the composition, Andre Kostelanetz, did their best to interpret the composer's language.

But the only authentic representation in the entire work was the sound of the whales. As the radio commentator said after the recording was over, "The whales played themselves." Because we don't know what one whale was trying to express to another, we can only accept at face value the commentator's remark and assume that the whales' communication fulfilled its own objective.

Of course we don't know for certain what Hovhaness wished to communicate either, but we can be sure that, given the fact of the artist's dilemma—the grandeur of inspiration and the failure of expression—Hovhaness's music as written down on his manuscript only approximates what he had heard in his head before he wrote it down. Furthermore, we know that the music, as it floods from strings, horns, woodwinds, and percussion on the stage at Lincoln Center, is only an approximation of what the conductor hoped to produce in imitation of what the composer himself had heard.

The American composer Charles Ives offers a similar example. According to Gilbert Highet, Ives "was not a stickler for exactitude. He felt that no single concert could ever express all he had in mind, and he would be content if the orchestra played with good will and came out approximately correct." In a very real sense, no matter how excellent a musical event, a play, an exhibition of paintings, or a novel may be, the truth is that, for the artist at least, it didn't *turn out.*

The reason, I believe, is that the artist isn't the Creator, the One who alone could look out upon all he had made and judge that it was very good. God the Creator engages in *poiesis,* the act of creating. It belongs solely to him. As men we are the agents of *mimesis,* the art of imitation. Yet through the lavishness of his common grace, we have been endowed with the prerogatives of creatures made in the image of God. We are invited to take the elements of his creation and rearrange them so that beauty may be seen in its many varied shapes and forms.

A complex vision lies dormant in the artist's unconscious, neither indexed nor catalogued in any verbal manner—nebulous, random, unnamed. Called forth mysteriously, this vision permeates the artist's imagination, memory, or dreams with such persistence as cannot be denied, until with an exhalation of joy, like a mother in her final pangs of delivery, the artist re-leases his vision in an objective form.

But he has not *created* in any primary or truly original sense. He has reshaped, reconstituted, redesigned. The artist transforms the reality of his vision into an abstraction nonetheless—that he hopes will somehow approximate the ideal beauty he has seen in his soul.

But to say that the artist doesn't create doesn't lead automati-cally to a cheap regard for art. No substance is more necessary to human welfare than art and no art more essential than the art of discourse between human beings. "Man cannot live on bread alone," said Jesus Christ; "he lives on every word that God utters" (Matthew 4:4). Among the utterances of God were his creative fiats, "Let there be." From the originating handiwork of God, man receives his warrant to bring art as well as nourish-ment into his being—the beauty of nature and of his imagination molded into new forms. Paul Claudel asked, "What is art, if not . . . a sort of mimicry of the Word that creates, the Word that is 'poetry,' a repeating of the *Fiat* which brought everything about?" And T. S. Eliot wrote, "The LORD who created must wish us to create / And employ our creation again in His service."

There is more, however, than beauty to be obtained from art. We have come to a point in history when the function of artists may well be to stand between us and self-destruction. Not be-cause artists today will succeed where prophets of doom in other empires have failed. The role of the writer as an artist of discourse is not the same as the role of a Cassandra, the Trojan princess doomed both to prophesy and not to be believed. In-stead the writer, along with all other true artists, will help to preserve human society against itself by doing what artists all along have been commissioned to do: "to hold, as 'twere, the mirror up to nature, to show virtue her own feature, scorn her own image, and the very age and body of the time his form and pressure." Or, as William Faulkner expressed it in his 1950 Nobel Prize acceptance speech,

> The poet's, the writer's, duty is . . . to help man endure by lifting his heart, by reminding him of the courage and honor and hope and pride and compassion and pity and sacrifice which have been the glory of his past. The poet's voice need not merely be the record of man, it can be one of the props, the pillars to help him endure and prevail.

The writer's responsibility is great; his problems are real indeed. To solve them, to begin solving them, he must turn to the great reservoir of his imagination, memory, and dreams—the domain of myth. Then through the vehicle of words he must try to come as close as possible to an expression of what he knows to be true. From time to time the grandeur of inspiration within the human spirit will break through the limits of language; as Longinus says, "Like a thunderbolt it carries all before it and reveals the writer's full power in a flash." At rare moments such as this, we do well to recognize the uniqueness of the event. Perhaps we'll then feel the need to take off our shoes, for the ground on which we stand is holy. But we'll also need to understand, with Nathaniel Hawthorne's artist of the Beautiful, that "the world . . . could never say the fitting word nor feel the fitting sentiment which should be the perfect recompense of an artist who . . . has won the beautiful into his handiwork." Perhaps the greatest lesson we can learn—whether as artists or as beneficiaries of their work—is that for the artist, as Hawthorne says, "the reward of all high performance must be sought within itself, or sought in vain."

Yet for any writer there sometimes arises a second dilemma, involving his sense of role in time and space, an ironic awareness of his limitations in the light of his apocalyptic responsibilities. Everyone who presumes to be a painter, a writer, a poet, takes upon himself the task of *composition*—the task of putting something together. That's what it means to *compose*. In the dying argot of the Aquarian Age, to compose is to get it together.

What is this *it* which the writer attempts to put together? Nothing less than his whole universe! When the writer decides to put words on paper, he has made a rigorous decision regarding the state of affairs around him. He has decided that, for whatever reasons, something more permanent than vocal talk is needed. He might have gone so far as to carve out another Mount Rushmore, but for his purposes a pencilled poem will do. He has decided to make his statement, to organize the world in which he lives. Because he is truly serious, he has given some thought to what might seem the best of several alternatives by which to convince his reader of the validity of his vision. He has the highest possible sense of purpose, and he molds the elements around him in a conscious, deliberate decision to compose, to get his universe into an orderly shape.

Then a doubt may strike through to him—a crippling doubt about the universe out there. In fragments, so broken and splintered by corruption, mendacity, and greed, its best description may be Huckleberry Finn's: "I never seen anybody but lied, one time or another." Perhaps the universe, like Humpty Dumpty, can never be put together again; perhaps it has gone its reckless way, an asteroid of infinitesimal insignificance lost in the sidereal expanse. Perhaps there is nothing to compose.

At this same moment the writer may feel the pulse of a related fearfulness, that to compose the universe may mean coming to grips with himself and with the disorder of his own life. He may discover some matters in his life that he prefers not to put down on paper, even under the guise of fiction. His reasons will not be restricted to maintaining privacy; instead, the real hindrance will be his apprehension that those words on paper might forever shape his universe around them. As long as his experience remains ephemeral, unexpressed by the permanence of words, it also remains an abstraction.

No aspiring artist can allow this dilemma to persist unresolved. Wishing to compose, yet afraid of what his composition might turn out to be, he must nonetheless write what is in him. The history of so-called confessional literature, from St. Augustine's *Confessions* and continuing to the present in novels and autobiographies, tells us that there is more than merely getting a load off one's chest to be gained from controlled introspection. There is also the likelihood of cleansing and renewal; there is the probability that the writer will emerge from an honest encounter with himself and his universe a better man.

All this depends, of course, upon the writer's ability to keep in balance his view of himself and his relationship to the universe of which he is but a part. His experience is limited, his imagination may seem unduly circumscribed by that narrow experience. But this is true of every man until he learns to step out of himself, as it were, and gains a perspective on his role as one of the mainstays of mankind's survival. The best illustration I know of such a balanced view may be heard in the voice of Black Elk, the Oglala Sioux holy man, whose life-narrative begins:

My friend, I am going to tell you the story of my life, as you wish;
and if it were only the story of my life I think I would not tell it; for
what is one man that he should make much of his winters, even
when they bend him like a heavy snow? So many other men have
lived and shall live that story, to be grass upon the hills.

It is the story of all life that is holy and is good to tell, and of us
two-leggeds sharing it with the four-legged and the wings of the air
and all green things; for these are children of one mother and their
father is one Spirit.

This, then, is not the tale of a great hunter or of a great warrior, or
of a great traveler, although I have made much meat in my time and
fought for my people both as boy and man, and have gone far and
seen strange lands and men. So also have many others done, and
better than I. These things I shall remember by the way, and often
they may seem to be the very tale itself, as when I was living them
in happiness and sorrow. But now that I see it all as from a lonely
hilltop, I know it was the story of a mighty vision given to a man too
weak to use it; of a holy tree that should have flourished in a people's
heart with flowers and singing birds, and now is withered; and of a
people's dream that died in bloody snow.

But if the wisdom was true and mighty, as I know, it is true and
mighty yet; for such things are of the spirit, and it is in the darkness
of their eyes that men get lost.

The greatest writers have always comprehended in fullness
a vision that is "true and mighty yet." They have also pointed
out with unfailing regularity that man's lost condition is the
result of his own spiritual blindness, the result of a failure to
see! Sophocles' Oedipus is, as Bernard Knox calls him, "a paradigm of all mankind"—proud, self-sufficient, relentless in pur-
suing his own downfall, blinded by arrogant ignorance. In the
same manner Albert Camus' Jean-Baptiste Clamence, narrator
of *The Fall*, represents modern man in his desperate search for
reprieve from the condemnation of his own conscience. Near
the end of his monologue, Clamence says, "I'm like that old
beggar who wouldn't let go of my hand one day on a cafe ter-
race: 'Oh sir,' he said, 'it's not just that I'm no good, but you
lose track of the light.'"

Many honest men today would claim the old beggar's self-
description for themselves. Many of us have lost track of the
light, in spite of the attempts of some among us to find what
Arthur Miller calls "illumination of the ethical." Most of our
artists, Miller says, "have given up trying to search out the right
way of living."

But among the great writers are also those who have seen a
more transcendent vision of man—man redeemed and restored

to his original relationship with God through the atonement of Jesus Christ. These are Christian writers whose theme is the triumphant cry of St. Paul in the midst of his despair: "Miserable creature that I am, who is there to rescue me out of this body doomed to death? God alone, through Jesus Christ our Lord! Thanks be to God!" (Romans 7:24-25).

The Christian writer is an artist who brings the life of Christ to his art, enhancing it with the brilliance of faith, the warmth of love, the certitude of hope. Such a vision affects his art, giving him a new perspective on the human situation because he now sees it with the help of divine illumination. W. H. Auden suggests how a Christian outlook may affect the art of drama:

> Greek tragedy is the tragedy of necessity: i.e., the feeling aroused in the spectator is "What a pity it had to be this way"; Christian tragedy is the tragedy of possibility, "What a pity it was this way when it might have been otherwise."

This century has witnessed numerous gifted writers whose art has been integrated with an unalloyed personal commitment to Jesus Christ. Several of them have won the Nobel Prize for Literature, including T. S. Eliot, Pär Lagerkvist, Francois Mauriac, Boris Pasternak, and Aleksandr Solzhenitsyn. The names of C. S. Lewis, Charles Williams, J. R. R. Tolkien, Alan Paton, and Graham Greene are known to readers throughout the world. Among American writers the most prominent professing Christians in recent years have been Flannery O'Connor, Marianne Moore, John Updike, W. H. Auden, Frederick Buechner, Edmund Fuller, and D. Keith Mano.

These and other Christian writers share the knowledge that their art receives its living, lasting quality from a source beyond imagination, memory, or dreams. The late Flannery O'Connor said, "The Christian writer particularly will feel that whatever his initial gift is, it comes from God." The Christian writer's vision is a commissioning from God. To Habakkuk God said, "Write down the vision" (Habakkuk 2:2); to the Apostle John he said, "Write down therefore what you have seen, what is now, and what will be hereafter" (Revelation 1:19). In this sense the Christian writer agrees with Stanley Burnshaw's observation, that "the poet knows . . . he is *being used*." In the strictest terms of Christian vocation, the Christian writer has been called to be used in telling other men that the Word, the Divine *Logos*, became flesh in the Person of Jesus Christ.

The Christian writer knows, moreover, why the Word became flesh—to become the Liberating Word, the Word that sets men free. In his first recorded sermon, at the synagogue in Nazareth, Jesus read a passage from Isaiah's prophecy, then made an astonishing personal claim:

> The spirit of the Lord is upon me because he has anointed me; he has sent me to announce good news to the poor, to proclaim release for prisoners and recovery of sight for the blind; to let the broken victims go free, to proclaim the year of the Lord's favor. (Luke 4:18-19)

Then he closed the book and said, "Today in your very hearing this text has come true." For this claim his townspeople tried to kill him.

What had Jesus done to provoke such violence? He had announced himself as the Messiah, the Anointed of God, the object of divine choice, the personification of Israel's greatest vision. He had claimed the indwelling and illumination of the Holy Spirit. He had also declared that his divine message was "good news." And what was that good news, that gospel? Release of prisoners, restoration for the helpless, freedom for the broken victims of oppression: in short, *liberation!* All this the young prophet from Nazareth promised.

To those who believe in him, all this the Son of God—the Liberating Word—fulfills in setting men free. The artist who believes this message has the opportunity of passing on to others the Word that releases men from enshackling sin, that dissolves the fetters of hatred, prejudice, pride, and greed. God the Creator has made men as his *handiwork,* his *poem* says the Greek (Ephesians 2:10). Those who believe the Word are to become the Word, the only Word some men may understand—spokesmen for the gospel, rhetoricians of the divine mystery.

CHAPTER TWO

making known the mystery

The love of mystery is a universal human trait. The favorite tales of our childhood are stories of the unknown, the strange, the unpredictable, the catastrophic; in a word, the *mystery*. "That's scary!" my little girl says with a shudder, but the look on her face convinces me of her delight. The best rides at Disneyland are those whose complete route can't be seen from the ticket booth.

"Man is so made," said Arthur Machen, "that all his true delight arises from the contemplation of mystery." The ultimate mystery is ourselves, and to solve that mystery we ask the great questions of identity, purpose, destiny: Who am I? Where did I come from? Why am I here? Where am I going?

Most attempts at probing the mystery of human existence have led men eventually to look for a relationship between religion and life. Art and ritual celebrations attempt to express such a relationship. For example, most ancient civilizations found a similarity between the cycle of the seasons and the passage from one stage of life to another. This led them to establish rituals and sacraments growing out of their reverence for the dimly realized truth.

The Greeks called their ceremonies *mysteries*. Here they perpetuated a religious and cultural ethic based on the retelling, in generation after generation, of stories derived from myth. But the purpose of these rites was not to solve the mystery being celebrated; instead, the Greek celebrant regarded the mystery as inscrutable, something to be held in awe.

The most famous of the mysteries, held at Eleusis, provides an illustration worth noting. Most of the concrete details of the Eleusinian Mysteries remain shrouded in antiquity, but we do know that Eleusis, situated between Athens and the Corinthian isthmus, was a center for the worship of Demeter, goddess of the earth. According to myth, Demeter's daughter Persephone had been carried off by Hades, god of the underworld, to be his wife. Demeter's grieving search for her lost child brought her to Eleusis, where she was well received and a temple built in her honor. During the period of Demeter's sorrow, no grain had grown, but when Persephone was at last restored to Demeter, the earth-goddess caused crops once more to grow.

To the Greeks this story of tragic loss and rapturous reunion meant more than just the equivalent of a human child's being lost then found. Persephone as daughter of the goddess of the earth represented all that grows, dies and disappears, then is reborn. To the Greek mind, the Demeter and Persephone story blended natural conditions of agriculture with the phenomena of death and resurrection. By participating in the mystery rites, the Greek hoped for a unifying experience that would make his body and mind at one with his soul—not unlike the experience of the Christian who celebrates the sacrifice of Jesus Christ by partaking of bread and wine.

It was this larger spiritual concept, transcending a mere seasonal festival, that was commemorated at Eleusis. Yet the mysteries weren't open to the public; they belonged only to the initiated, to those who had passed through secret rites of baptism, prayer, singing, dancing, and certain undisclosed climactic ceremonies within the shrine.

Scholars assure us that the mysteries began long before any possible historical dating, so deeply runs the core of man's concern with matters beyond his comprehending. Joseph Campbell says, "The ultimate origins of the wild rites are lost in the depths of an unrecorded past: indeed, . . . they are certainly very much older than the history, or even the prehistory, of Greece itself." The poet John Keats saw this timelessness in the beauty of a Grecian vase and wrote,

> Thou, silent form, dost tease us out of thought
> As doth eternity.

It shouldn't surprise us, then, to find that when the Apostle Paul wished to refer to the ageless and unfathomable truths of his faith in Jesus Christ, he used the word *mysterion*. In using this word a score of times, Paul wasn't equating Christianity with the pagan mysteries. Instead he was relying upon the word's familiarity to his Hellenic and Roman audiences, particularly for its connotations of exclusiveness. To the Mediterranean mind, a *mysterion* was a secret known only to the initiated.

Unlike the mystery at Eleusis, however, the mystery of God was not to be kept hidden. To the Romans Paul wrote,

> Now to him who is able to strengthen you according to my gospel and the preaching of Jesus Christ, according to the revelation of the mystery which was kept secret for long ages but is now disclosed and through the prophetic writings is made known to all nations, according to the command of the eternal God, to bring about the obedience of faith — to the only wise God be glory for evermore through Jesus Christ! Amen. (Romans 16:25-27)

Paul asked that the Ephesians pray for him, whose mission was "to make known the mystery of the gospel" (Ephesians 6:19, KJV). To the Corinthians Paul likened himself to an official in charge of a sacred ritual, calling himself one of the "stewards of the mysteries of God" (1 Corinthians 4:1, RSV). And to Timothy Paul spelled out that mystery in clearest terms: "Great indeed, we confess, is the mystery of our religion: He was manifested in the flesh, vindicated in the Spirit, seen by angels, preached among the nations, believed on in the world, taken up in glory" (1 Timothy 3:16, RSV).

Paul came to know the mystery of the gospel by *revelation*, as his letters in several instances declare. This revelation began with a shocking vision of the Resurrected Christ and continued as an illumination of the Law and the Prophets, which as a Pharisee he knew so well. Paul didn't unravel the mystery himself; he received enlightenment from a source outside himself, for such is the very nature of revelation. To the Galatians he wrote, "I must make it clear to you, my friends, that the gospel you heard me preach is no human invention. I did not take it from any man; no man taught it me; I received it through a revelation of Jesus Christ" (Galatians 1:11-12).

The source of Paul's revelation, his illumination into the mystery of the gospel, was the Spirit of God; so he says in his letter to the Ephesians: "When you read this you can perceive my insight into the mystery of Christ, which was not made known to the sons of men in other generations as it has now been revealed to his holy apostles and prophets by the Spirit" (Ephesians 3:4-5, RSV).

The Spirit enlightened Paul to the mystery of Christ, the

mystery of the gospel, thereby making Paul one of the initiated. Such has always been the function of the Spirit within the Divine Trinity. The Spirit is Light, the "Eternal coeternal beam," as John Milton wrote. Elsewhere Paul rhapsodizes on the same theme: "For the same God who said, 'Out of darkness let light shine,' has caused his light to shine within us, to give the light of revelation—the revelation of the glory of God in the face of Jesus Christ" (2 Corinthians 4:6).

This quotation takes us back where we belong when we start discussing God—back to the very beginning of beginnings, back to Creation itself. Two passages from the Bible, the first chapter of Genesis and the first chapter of the Gospel according to John, give us the classic biblical statements.

> In the beginning of creation, when God made heaven and earth, the earth was without form and void, with darkness over the face of the abyss, and a mighty wind that swept over the surface of the waters. God said, "Let there be light," and there was light. (Genesis 1:1-3)
> When all things began, the Word already was. The Word dwelt with God, and what God was, the Word was. The Word, then, was with God at the beginning, and through him all things came to be; no single thing was created without him. All that came to be was alive with his life, and that life was the light of men. The light shines on in the dark, and the darkness has never mastered it. (John 1:1-5)

These two passages construct the basis upon which Milton wrote, in *Paradise Lost*,

> Heaven opened wide
> . . . .
> . . . . to let forth
> The King of Glory, in his powerful Word
> And Spirit coming to create new worlds.
>   (Book VII, 205-209)

The preexistent God transcends time, dimension, and description. He is One, recognizable by the singularity of his will and the diversity of his character. The Hebrew word used for God in Genesis 1 is *Elohim*, a plural form. The plural pronouns *us* and *our* also appearing in this chapter confirm the suggestion of diversity. But the acts of God confirm his *Divine Volition*. He is the God who wills the creation of a universe *ex nihilo*, out of nothing, a universe beyond himself.

He is also the God whose glory and effulgence are Light itself. In the Genesis account of creation, we do not read that God *makes* the Light in the same way he *makes* the sun and moon, the fish and birds, or even man. Instead God wills that this

Light, which is the very glory of his presence, should shine: "Fiat lux!" This shining forth of light is the role of the Spirit of God in the mystery of creation, to be an expression of God's first gesture of love toward a chaotic void. This act of love was God's first act of common grace. Allan W. Watts writes,

> Love is said to be the unreserved pouring out, or giving away, of oneself for the good of another. It is that of which *shekinah*, the divine radiance, is primarily the symbol—for as the sun gives its light without reservation, and without asking anything in return, so God "maketh his sun to shine upon the evil and upon the good, and sendeth his rain upon the just and upon the unjust." It was by love, then, that God created the worlds, for when he gave to other things the power of life and existence, he gave them himself.

But more: St. John tells us that this same Light is "the real light which enlightens every man" (John 1:9). Thus God is not only Divine Volition, he is also *Divine Illumination*.

Furthermore, God is *Divine Communication*. According to John, the *Logos* or Word was coexistent with God. To the Word was granted the special task of creation. This is what the writer of Genesis means when he records that "God *said*." As Robert Farrar Capon points out, "The Word spoke the world into being."

The power of communication within the Godhead is fundamental to our understanding the mystery of the gospel. Everything that we know about identity, names, personhood, uniqueness, individual consciousness, and selfhood, we obtain from a knowledge that we were called into being. As we come to understand more and more about the immensity of the universe, the untold layers of primordial existence among various forms of life—mineral, vegetable, animal, and human—is it not all the more astounding that each of us has a name! When God the Word called palm trees, daffodils, crocodiles, and parakeets into existence, he first made each distinguishable, then commanded Man to subdue the earth. The first step toward subduing creation was for Man to call creation under his power by naming its parts. Though all else in Eden has been lost, men retain this one fragment of Paradise: When I was born, I was given a name by those whose love had called me into being.

I was also given a solemn reminder of my high place in the order of creation. For when God the Eternal Will summoned God the Eternal Light to shine, he spoke through God the Eternal Word. When the triune God created Man, he did so,

Genesis tells us, "in our image and likeness," meaning that God
permitted Man to share his own divine attributes of volition,
illumination, and communication. This is the *imago Dei*, the
image of God; God made Man able to exercise his will, to
choose; to perceive light from darkness, to reason; to express that
will and that reason in words, to speak.

The gift of language as conceptual communication is God's
everlasting testament to Man that Man is different from the
animals. Almost anything else we do, whether by choice, instinct,
or conditioned response, the oriole, the water buffalo, the but-
terfly, the German shepherd can do as well and sometimes
better. But language belongs to Man exclusively, and it is not for
nothing that we read, "So the Word became flesh." With Emily
Dickinson, we marvel at "this consent of Language / This loved
Philology."

The creative Word—in Hart Crane's phrase, the "Incogniz-
able Word / Of Eden"—becomes the knowable Incarnate Lord
in the person of Jesus Christ. The purpose of the Incarnation is
to continue his creating power by communicating directly with
men, as the writer to the Hebrews declares:

> When in former times God spoke to our forefathers, he spoke in frag-
> mentary and varied fashion through the prophets. But in this final
> age he has spoken to us in the Son whom he has made heir to the
> whole universe, and through whom he created all orders of existence.
> (Hebrews 1:1-2)

So far, we have explored the mystery of the gospel from its
source, from the point of God's willing the world into being, to
God's illumining the world into being, to God's speaking the
world into being. Thus the Trinity fulfills its complementary
functions, permeated throughout by the unifying characteristic
of Divine Love. But according to Scripture there is still more to
the mystery. The Son is the Word who creates by communication; he is also "the effulgence of God's splendor and the stamp
of God's very being." He is, as the statement of the Nicene Creed
avers, "God, of God: Light, of Light: Very God, of Very God."
The Son is the *Divine Expression* of God-ness.

He also sustains creation as the Divine Expression of will,
light, and word. The opening passage of the Epistle to the Hebrews goes on to say that "the Son . . . sustains the universe by
his word of power." Here the Greek word for *power* is *dynamis*,
from which we have the English word *dynamite*. A closer ren-

dering of *dynamis* in this context might be *omnipotent energy*. Through the energizing power of the Divine Word, what he calls into being he is also able to maintain in accordance with the Divine Will that ordained creation.

We have now been brought back full-circle to the place where we began—with revelation. The mystery of the gospel does not remain shut off from view; it is not limited to a tiny coterie of initiates. God wills that mankind should know and participate in the eternal mystery through the enlightenment of the Holy Spirit. The principal encounters between God and men, recorded in the Bible, demonstrate this truth. The Trinity collaborates in making known the abiding will of God through language and through light.

Consider, as an example, the experience of Moses. Driven by the violence of his actions from the life of a prince in the Pharaoh's court, he tends his father-in-law's herds on the far side of Jethro's property. Suddenly the incandescence of God's presence dances like fire before his eyes. Then he hears the Word speaking, "I AM; that is who I am," and the expression of Divine Will is given. Years later, having received the words of holy commandment and covenant on Mount Sinai, Moses returns to the Israelites, and his face shines with the brilliance of Divine Light: "He did not know that the skin of his face shone because he had been speaking with the Lord" (Exodus 34:29).

The calling of Isaiah illustrates the same principles at work. In his vision the young Isaiah sees the exalted God, enthroned and served by seraphic beings who perform his will. He is the King of Glory resplendent in holiness. He is also a purging fire, for a glowing coal from the altar burns away Isaiah's acknowledged sin. He is the Lord of the Word who speaks his will: "Then I heard the Lord saying, Whom shall I send? Who will go for me? And I answered, Here am I; send me. He said, Go and tell this people" (Isaiah 6:8-9).

On the Mount of Transfiguration, the dazzling Light of God's glory accompanies a spoken command, "This is my Son, my Chosen; listen to him" (Luke 9:35). The conversion of Saul of Tarsus on the Damascus road is another example. A blinding light, a voice, and the unmistakably clear volition of God:

> While he was still on the road and nearing Damascus, suddenly a light flashed from the sky all around him. He fell to the ground and heard a voice saying, "Saul, Saul, why do you persecute me?" "Tell

me, Lord," he said, "who you are." The voice answered, "I am Jesus, whom you are persecuting. But get up and go into the city, and you will be told what you have to do." (Acts 9:3-6)

On the island of Patmos, the aged Apostle John observed the same apocalyptic vision of threefold Light, Word, and Will—the figure of the resurrected Christ whose "face shone like the sun in full strength," whose "voice was like the sound of rushing waters," and whose will was to be obeyed (Revelation 1:12-16).

In each of these cases, as well as in others, *revelation* leads to *proclamation*. Moses does not remain a shepherd for Jethro. The sacred discourse does not remain locked in a top-secret drawer. The young visionary does not keep his message to himself. The inner circle of disciples do not withhold forever what they have seen. The blinded Pharisee does not stumble aimlessly into a foreign city. The imprisoned Apostle does not disobey the commandment to "write down . . . what you have seen" (Revelation 1:19). What these and others came to know, they also announced as "the secret meaning" (Revelation 1:20), the unfolding of God's truth. They were constrained to tell what they knew, "to proclaim the mystery of the gospel" (Ephesians 6:19, RSV).

                                    *   *   *

Borrowing from Marshall McLuhan, we can say that "the *mystery* is the message." The divine choice to enlighten the universe with the divine Word is the message communicated to every man. Furthermore, the mystery of Creation continues in the experience of each individual because, the Apostle John tells us, "the real light enlightens every man." To every man comes the singular moment of Creation power when God says, "Let there be light"—and there *is* light! Thereafter, through the bounty of common grace, each man participates, whether consciously or not, in the ongoing of God's creation.

A biblical understanding of Creation gives warrant to the belief, expressed by Denis de Rougement, that

> Christian meditation upon the act and the work of the artist can deepen, inform, and instruct itself within the framework of a meditation upon the doctrine and mystery of the Trinity; and that Christian meditation will find in the vocabulary and dialectical arguments employed for nearly twenty centuries by trinitarian theologians the whole of a theory which introduces us better than any other to the human mysteries of the act of art.

To return to the terms of the previous chapter, the artist is "being used" by the Trinity to the end that men might come to know God. The event of Creation wasn't static. True, God rested on the Seventh Day because he had "completed all the work he had been doing," and "because on that day he ceased from all the work he had set himself to do" (Genesis 2:2-3). But this wasn't the shutting down of the factory. It marked only the suspension of God's originating control, that power responsible for the creating of something from nothing. Once something had been created, God commanded its duplication and reduplication from within itself: "Let the earth produce fresh growth, let there be on the earth plants bearing seed, fruit-trees bearing fruit each with seed according to its kind" (Genesis 1:11; see also Genesis 1:24).

Part of the original creative act was to include in each living organism the desire and capacity to reproduce its own life and beauty. The process of pollenation and cross-fertilization in plants and trees correspond to mating urges in birds and animals. The same command also applied to Man, to whom God said, "Be fruitful and increase, fill the earth and subdue it" (Genesis 1:28). The command refers, of course, to progeny and the development of succeeding generations, but God's intention goes well beyond sexual reproduction. Because Man alone among the creatures possesses the quality of God's likeness, the image of God, Man alone owns the quality of judgment that allows him to perceive beauty. A compelling refrain throughout Genesis 1 is the writer's statement, "And God saw that it was good." The First Critic reaches a climax of praise in verse 31, "And God saw all that he had made, and it was very good."

The poet and scholar Chad Walsh has asked,

> Does the biblical doctrine of Creation hold an important key to the universality of esthetic activity and experience? It does seem odd that even the most "primitive" tribe, preoccupied with its daily survival, somehow finds time and energy to compose and transmit literature, to decorate baskets beyond functional requirements, to develop musical instruments. Does the *imago Dei* within us include an urge to carry on the work of creation?

When he summoned Man to "be fruitful and increase," God was issuing an invitation for Man to exercise more than merely the procreative energies given him—to reproduce the beauty he found all around him. Man had been placed in a beautiful environment, with "all trees pleasant to look at and good for food" (Genesis 2:9), with a companion to share his life—in short, a home where all was beauty. God gave Man none of his own omnipotence to create *ex nihilo,* but he did expect Man to arrange and rearrange the components of beauty in ever more pleasing form.

Man's first acts of artistry were as landscape gardener and poet. But Adam hadn't created the plants, shrubs, and trees in Eden; he merely tilled and tended them. He hadn't made the marvelous new being brought before him; he merely found himself overwhelmingly stirred to care for her as for no other being, so stirred that he broke out in lyric verse,

> Now this, at last—
> bone from my bones,
> flesh from my flesh! —

the first love-song!

God the Creator, Man the artificer of that creation. "All good giving, every perfect gift, comes from above," the Apostle James writes, "from the Father of the lights of heaven" (James 1:17). In spite of the Fall, God hasn't suspended his commission for men to be artists. The doctrine of common grace applies here. Common grace is the favor of God upon his entire Creation, showing itself in the power that restrains evil, that causes the sun to shine, the rain to fall, whether men are righteous or unrighteous. God's grace upon all men demonstrates his concern for everything he has made, but God's goodness carries further still, continuing to imbue men with gifts of illumination and expression. A man may make of that gift whatever he chooses, and in choosing he may even reject the very light by which he sees.

Friedrich Nietzsche, for example, is as much an heir to God's common grace as, say, Mozart, who believed his genius to be a "gift I have my Divine Maker to thank for." Nietzsche also accepted a theory of artistic inspiration from an external source, claiming that "one can hardly reject completely the idea that one is the mere incarnation, or mouthpiece, or medium of some almighty power." But what did each artist do with his gift of common grace? It is impossible to listen to Mozart without experiencing an elevation of spirit. Nietzsche's legacy is entirely different. In spite of the ecstasy of which he writes—an exhilaration felt during the composition of *Thus Spoke Zarathustra*— the result of Nietzsche's inspiration is a vision of the world distorted by denial. Here is a typically Nietzschean sentiment:

"What is the greatest thing you can experience? It is the hour of the great contempt. The hour in which even your happiness grows loathsome to you, and your reason and virtue also."

Or, this passage from *The Antichrist*:

What is good? Everything that heightens the feeling of power in man, the will to power, power itself.
What is bad? Everything born of weakness.
What is happiness? The feeling that power is *growing,* that resistance is overcome.
Not contentedness but more power; not peace but war; not virtue but fitness. . . .
The weak and the failures shall perish: first principle of *our* love of man. And they shall be given every possible assistance.
What is more harmful than any vice? Active pity for all the failures and all the weak: Christianity.

Little wonder that Adolf Hitler used some of the writings of his countryman—out of philosophical context, to be sure—as a call to "the Master-Race" and its mission to eliminate the world's weaklings!

The artist receives from God's common grace the originating influences of the Trinity upon all Creation. Now, as then, the Will of God impels him to speak out of recesses too profound to fathom. "It is in me and shall out," says the poet. This profundity of our being is that same vast unknown region of imagination, memory, and dreams—the sphere within where resides the human spirit; the stimulus to faith, to love, to the eternal mystery by which we order our lives.

The Light of God illumines these depths of our spirit by reasoning, by metaphor, by analogy.

> Too bright for our infirm Delight
> The Truth's superb surprise,

wrote Emily Dickinson, showing the poet's recognition that her art could best reveal the truth by indirection. Because of the Light's surpassing brilliance,

> The Truth must dazzle gradually
> Or every man be blind.

Then the Word of God, the elemental creative Word, converts this inexpressible Light into a rhetoric sublimely true. The poet John Dryden illustrates the artist's nebulous awareness of this threefold stimulus to creative passion. In his dedicatory "To the Right Honorable Roger, Earl of Orrery," Dryden speaks of

the earliest stages of composition as "only a confused mass of
thoughts, tumbling over one another in the dark." The impulse
to write was present but without illumination. Later he felt
his "fancy" or imagination "moving the sleeping images of things
towards the light." Finally Dryden sensed a point of conscious
verbal discrimination, "there to be distinguished, and then either
chosen or rejected by the judgment."

In this act of discrimination the artist exercises his responsibilities granted through common grace. Exiled from Eden, he
nonetheless has been summoned to keep nature under his order-
ing, to name its parts, to preserve what remains of its beauty.
He can do so either for good or for evil, either to honor his commission or to desecrate even further the Garden of God.

The artist who is a writer has a particular responsibility for the
gift of language. He must comprehend its power, its flexibility,
its adaptability to new circumstances, its maintenance of tradition through connotation. In choosing his language, the writer
reveals his vision and shows the scope of his gift. The art of
writing, as stunning as it may be in the hands of some few
persons, has inherent limitations. It is almost wholly insufficient
to encompass the ideas behind it. Words are not in themselves
reality but only the written signs and articulated sounds that
suggest certain qualities about reality: We can never express
how much we love her or hate him; we can never convey how
profoundly we are moved by beauty or grief. Yet with T. S.
Eliot's Sweeney, the writer knows, "I gotta use words when
I talk to you."

But the writer refuses to yield to frustration. He must try. He
has been blessed by a compelling gift. He can't abandon his
vision or forsake the use of language because he thinks himself
an inadequate spokesman. For him writing is what Milton called
"that one talent which is death to hide." He must learn to use
language in the most felicitous, most effective way possible. He
must learn to appreciate and discriminate among words, *words*,
WORDS. One word is not the same as another, and there is no
such thing as an exact synonym: *red* is not *scarlet*, *high* is not
lofty, *war* is not *carnage*, *affection* is not *love*.

"The difference," said Mark Twain, "between the right word
and the nearly right word is the difference between *lightning*
and the *lightning bug*." Or as Professor Emile Cailliet puts it,

As every writer worth his salt very well knows, there is only one specific, irreplaceable term that fits into a certain situation. It is the knack of hitting upon such terms continually, often by dint of laborious effort, which distinguishes the great stylist and helps dress the truth in beautiful garb. And this is, properly, the function of the artist.

To "dress the truth in beautiful garb" is the function of the artist; to "adorn the doctrine of God" (Titus 2:10, RSV) is the function of the Christian artist. His mandate comes through common grace, the same as to every man. He understands that in granting men the privilege of participating in an ongoing creation, God intends thereby to reveal himself more and more. This he has done since the beginning, as Paul contends:

> For all that may be known of God by men lies plain before their eyes; indeed God himself has disclosed it to them. His invisible attributes, that is to say his everlasting power and deity, have been visible, ever since the world began, to the eye of reason, in the things he has made. (Romans 1:19-20)

In God's dominion we find no arbitrary division between so-called sacred and secular objects. Nothing in nature can be profane, because God has called it "good." Likewise nothing shaped by man, unless its specific intent is to rob God of his splendor, can be categorized as "secular." Beethoven's quartets are no more secular than Bach's cantatas; Copland's "Appalachian Spring" is as sacred as Berlioz' oratorio *L'Enfance du Christ.* The same applies, with the same qualification, to composition in other forms. The Christian has received no warrant from God to classify any expression of beauty as less than sacred. Through nature, through the arts, through life, God makes himself known. As the English Jesuit poet Gerard Manley Hopkins says,

> Christ plays in ten thousand places,
> Lovely in limbs, and lovely in eyes not his
> To the Father through the features of men's faces.

But the Christian writer has also experienced the mandate under special grace, the grace of redemption made necessary by sin, made possible by love. "For you know the grace of our Lord Jesus Christ," says St. Paul, "that though he was rich, yet for your sake he became poor, so that by his poverty you might become rich" (2 Corinthians 8:9, RSV). The Christian writer carries this message. He also knows what Paul Claudel meant when he wrote,

> What a responsibility for us writers, above all, who are the leaders

of men and the directors of their souls! The mere fact of our enlightenment makes us spread light all about us. We are delegated by the
rest of the world to the way of knowledge and truth, and there is no
other truth but Christ, who is the Way and the Life, and the duty of
knowing and serving Him lies more heavily on us than upon others,
and lies upon us with a terrible urgency.

The Christian writer's duty is to make known the mystery, to
order and arrange language in a manner that glorifies the Giver
of his gift. For his purpose, the Christian writer has at his
command the whole battery of language. In his vision on
Patmos, the Apostle John heard the Resurrected Word declare,
"I am the Alpha and the Omega" (Revelation 1:8). Not only
is Christ the Word, but also the very alphabet!

According to the 18th-century English poet Christopher
Smart, the letters of the alphabet themselves are emblems of
God. Sent to Bedlam for his supposed madness, Smart knew
what his keepers did not: that the Lord of Creation, the Living
Word, is also Lord over every jot and tittle, every dotted *i* and
crossed *t*, in the language of praise. Smart's poem "Jubilate
Agno," an expanded paraphrase of Psalms 148 and 150, calls
for praise from

> Nations, and languages, and every Creature
> in which is the breath of life.
> . . . .
> For H is a spirit and therefore he is God.
> For K is king and therefore he is God.
> For L is love and therefore he is God.
> For M is musick and therefore he is God.

As praise is offered, Smart tells us, men hear in return,

> Hallelujah from the heart of God,
> and from the hand of the artist inimitable.

The writer, the artist, who thus engages in a divine exchange
of beauty with the Creator of beauty himself will also perceive
what Hopkins meant when he wrote,

> Beyond saying sweet, past telling of the tongue,
> Thou art lightning and love.

CHAPTER THREE

myth and christian reality

From antiquity the poet's role has been to transmit to other men the revelation of God; as Milton said, "to justify the ways of God to man." This revelation itself is common and available to all men; but the capacity to transmit its beauty belongs to the artist. Ralph Waldo Emerson called the poet's special gift "an ulterior intellectual perception."

Emerson's "perception" is what I've been referring to as the artist's vision. So far I've made only a vague connection between this vision and the writer's imagination or his recollective faculties of memory or dreams. I've claimed that God is the source of artistic inspiration, that he fills the reservoir of the spirit from which the painter or poet draws his own particular stimulus to fashion the Beautiful. But what is it that fills the reservoir? What makes up the writer's vision?

The answer I offer is simple enough; I can say it in a single word: *myth*. The explanation takes a little more effort and space. Let's begin by noting that scarcely two people on earth will agree on a definition of *myth*. The problem of finding a satisfactory theoretical definition is complicated by the popular misuse of the word as a synonym for *misconception, fallacy, delusion,* or even *lie*. Sloppy editorial writers inveigh against "the *myth* of Federal aid" when they mean "the *mistaken idea* that the Federal government will pay the bill." Tourist handbooks refer to "the *mythical* Loch Ness monster" or "the *mythical* Abominable Snowman," meaning that these creatures are really nonexistent.

Such usage is a corruption of *myth*, which has no connection with falsehood, deception, or error. To begin to understand the essential integrity of myth and its discreteness from falsehood, it is necessary to make a clear distinction between *myth* and *mythology,* or between myth and the collections of myths in books like Bullfinch or Edith Hamilton or Gayley's *Classic Myths.* The same is true of the ancient works such as Ovid's *Metamorphoses* or even Hesiod's *Theogony,* the earliest known Greek account of Creation and the families of the gods.

From these books, from Homer's *Iliad* and *Odyssey,* from Germany's *Nibelungenlied* and Iceland's *Elder Edda,* we learn the story side of myth. From this important dimension we gain lasting connotations of splendor and folly experienced by the deities of Olympus or Asgard, as well as by mere mortals; we gain tales of heroic deeds and of intervention by the gods in the affairs of men. We also find prescientific explanations for various wonders in the order of nature. All this comes to us as mythological narrative, the work of poets and singers derived from the same sort of experience with imagination, memory, and dreams that produces fiction and drama today. These works were recognized in their own time as fictions. The Greek philosopher Xenophanes, who lived in the late 6th and early 5th centuries B. C., criticized Hesiod and Homer for their anthropomorphized view of the gods and especially for attributing to them "all that is a shame and a reproach among men—theft, adultery, deceit and other lawless acts."

Mythology isn't myth. Mythology is man's attempt at decoding the mysterious and making it a rational system, with a hierarchy like his own. Mythology is a deterioration to absurdity of primordial truth, the truth of myth. What was this earlier truth now debased in stories, say, of Zeus's infidelity and Hera's jealousy? How can we, at this distant remove in time, reconstruct it? The honest answer, of course, is that we can't reconstruct completely any original myth. But we can obtain glimmerings of what its glory once was, and from that spark of light we can proceed.

For our best historical source we return to the mystery rites. Many classicists and cultural anthropologists agree that myth is inextricably tied to religious ritual. Not all agree as to which came first, the myth or the ritual, the ritual or the myth. But it seems clear from the research of Jane E. Harrison, Gilbert Murray, S. H. Hooke, Lord Raglan, Bronislaw Malinowski, and Walter F. Otto, to name only a few of the prominent scholars, that myth is the verbal narrative (*mythos* in Greek means "story") of that event which ritual attempts to reenact.

The underlying purpose of ancient mystery rites was to find answers to man's most pressing questions about himself. This search led man to look outside himself, beyond the confines of his own being, to investigate the quality and characteristics of the greater Being he inferred from the inexplicable awe he felt whenever confronted by silhouettes of supremacy in nature.

Did man's search then result in his concocting stories to explain the phenomena that frightened him? Or did he first invest his daily routine with a pattern of repeated gestures which he later recognized as necessary to his well-being? Then later still, did he develop an accompanying narrative to explain the necessity and good sense—indeed, the religious obligation—of his rite?

Many scholars address themselves to this problem. A sampler of quotations may be useful. First, Malinowski:

> Myth fulfills in primitive culture an indispensable function; it expresses, enhances, and codifies belief; it safeguards and enforces morality; it vouches for the efficiency of ritual and contains practical rules for the guidance of man. Myth is thus a vital ingredient of human civilization; it is not an idle tale, but a hard-worked active force; it is not an intellectual explanation or an artistic imagery, but a pragmatic charter of primitive faith and moral wisdom.

Malinowski then goes on to say that "myth comes into play when rite, ceremony, or a social or moral rule demands justification, warrant of antiquity, reality, and sanctity."

Hooke offers this explanation: "The original myth, inseparable in the first instance from its ritual, embodies in more or less symbolic fashion, the original situation which is seasonally re-enacted in the ritual." Elsewhere Hooke writes:

> Together with the ritual and as an essential part of it there was always found, in some form or other, the recitation of the story whose outlines were enacted in the ritual. This was the myth, and its repetition had equal potency with the performance of the ritual. In the beginning the thing said and the thing done were inseparably united.

Finally, Otto says this: "That the true myth is not without its ritual is shown in that it in itself is a recital, a kind of ritual act. The myth is, as the Greeks designated it, the 'word'—that is to say, it is what it is only in a spoken form." But the mythos must be something extraordinary, something more powerful than our common usage of language reveals. Otto then says,

> It must be the kind of word which not merely designates the thing,

but *is* the thing itself. . . . If the word *is* the thing itself, in a manner which, of course, simply remains incomprehensible to the rational, scholarly way of thinking, then it cannot be but that it is effective in the realm of things. And of this kind is the word of the myth which the ancient peoples designated as the true one.

Something of the magnitude of the scholar's problem in explaining myth may be realized from the struggle of these writers, among many, to convey what they intuitively know. I suggest, however, one reason for the breakdown of the scholar's thesis: It is uniformly one-sided; it deals exclusively with *man's* attempts to establish a means of answering his questions through myth and ritual. The Christian sees a different answer to questions concerning myth and worship, an answer that takes into account the existence of a personal God. The Christian believes that while man searched, he was also *being sought*. God, not man, initiated the relationship between deity and humanity; God instilled in man a desire to know himself, his Creator, and the Creation of which he was a part.

Myth is far from being either fabulous falsehood or even what Malinowski calls "a narrative resurrection of a primeval reality, told in satisfaction of deep religious wants." Ultimately myth is God-made rather than man-made; ultimately true, ultimately good, because God creates no less than true and good. Furthermore, myth was created by God to serve three glorious and effective purposes: first, to be one of the means, before the Incarnation, of revealing himself and his sovereignty; second, to be a means of preserving the knowledge of himself among all peoples of the world, however faint that knowledge may grow; and third, to be an eternal wellspring that fills the reservoir of imagination, memory, and dreams, from which men may draw their impulse to compose something beautiful.

To find the source of myth, we must look farther than most anthropologists or myth scholars care to search. We must extend our conception of reality beyond any boundaries of time. History antedates mankind's recorded knowledge of himself, whether we date that knowledge from Upper Paleolithic cave art found at Lascaux or from Professor Leakey's "Homo habilis," about 1,800,000 years ago. History in its largest sense begins in eternity with the sublimity of the Mind of God and the co-eternal Trinity. But history as we know it, in the form of daily journals and accounts of human decisions, doesn't begin among various cultures and ethnic groups until approximately five thousand years ago—an infinitesimal flash in time.

This chasm of incalculable aeons between the eternal sphere and verifiable human history is, in Roy Harvey Pearce's term, "transhistorical," bridged only by myth. "Beyond history," he says, "there is myth, and then—but only then—God's Word." The creative energy of the Divine Word, which called Creation into being, is the same Word interacting with that Creation in history. It follows, therefore, that the bridge between God in eternity and men in history should be that same ineffable Word, inexpressible as Myth but fully known as the Incarnate Lord. Thus Myth and Christian Reality are One.

Since the Incarnation, God has required that those who would come to know him recognize "the revelation of the glory of God in the face of Jesus Christ." Since the Incarnation, God has been "in Christ reconciling the world to himself" (2 Corinthians 5:19). Since the Incarnation, the primary means of revelation are through the Person of Jesus Christ in the experience of the apostles, recorded for us in the New Testament, and through the personal indwelling of the Spirit of God in all believers. Wherever this message is told, it becomes the Christian Reality superseding myth because, as we shall see, the Incarnation of the Word in Jesus of Nazareth makes possible the complete fulfillment of promises contained in myth.

But the God who created time out of eternity is therefore the God of history, and all his dealings with men are acts along the continuum of human history. Myth and the mythic mode of expression—what scholars call "literary myth"—remain historically important even though myth is now a limited and secondary method of divine revelation. Myth is still important because we today may look back, in the pages of Scripture, and learn of experiences belonging to men of earliest ages, particularized in the Hebrew stories of Genesis 1-11.

These stories belong to God. He is the Author and he has placed them in a realm of human consciousness so deeply buried that neither history nor art can fathom them. They comprise the prologue to the epic of God and men; they are therefore impossible to ignore. Furthermore the fact that these stories exist as myth—as condensed, poetic expressions of unimaginable, inexpressible truth—is itself a necessary consequence of the Fall of Man, the pivotal event they narrate. Had Man remained obedient to God, had there been no expulsion from Eden, there would have been no reason for Adam's sons to know God only indirectly.

Before the Fall, Man knew no separation from God and had no need to interpret the reality of a daily presence, the oneness of Creator and creature. Man had no need for myth. Then that union was severed; the consequences of disobedience followed— exile, murder, immorality, judgment, and the widening separation even of men from each other through dispersion and foreign languages. These are the phases of human experience known to us in Genesis as the killing of Abel by Cain, the wickedness in the days of Noah, the Flood, the Tower of Babel.

Once Man's concord with God had been ruined, it became only an indistinct recollection. Man needed a permanent, indelible reminder of that presence and power now lost to him. Through common grace God provided this reminder in the form of myth, the public memory of all nations. This memory recalls in us all primary human experiences which in our lives are but reenactments. From the mythic consciousness of what once was ours we derive that sense of restlessness and estrangement anywhere but at our heart's home. The Germans call it *Sehnsucht*; our term is *homesickness*, but C. S. Lewis (to whose clarity on this whole difficult matter I'm indebted) speaks of it as "our inconsolable secret":

> The sense that in this universe we are treated as strangers, the longing to be acknowledged, to meet with some response, to bridge some chasm that yawns between us and reality, is part of our inconsolable secret. . . . Our life-long nostalgia, our longing to be reunited with something in the universe from which we now feel cut off, to be on the outside, is no mere neurotic fancy, but the truest index of our real situation.

When Man left Eden, he lost what was; he also lost his knowledge of what *had been*. He left behind whatever rights of intimacy with God he had known. He was no longer privy to daily communion with his Maker. If there had ever been the need for questions, Man had but to ask in order to receive authoritative answers. Now these were cut off. Man entered upon the truly Dark Ages, ages when God withheld from most men the total reality of his presence. From the Fall through the story of the prideful Tower, God's dealings with men grew more and more remote. The exceptions in Genesis are Cain, upon whom God placed his mark (Genesis 4:15); the mysterious

Enoch who "walked with God," then suddenly "was seen no more, because God had taken him away" (Genesis 5:24); and Noah. The God known to Adam by his voice became a distant power known only by his wrath. But the sons of Adam retained some faint memory of Eden which throughout the aeons became known as myth.

This is the Hebrew version found in Genesis 1-11. The myth scholar Joseph Campbell confirms that "comparative cultural studies have now demonstrated beyond question that similar mythic tales are to be found in every quarter of this earth." In other words, implanted in mankind's memory is the universal story of a creation and of a fall from primary bliss. The source of this implantation, I repeat, is God himself, who will not let Man's memory die.

But if, as Campbell claims, the Hebrew myth of Creation, the Garden of Eden, the Fall, the Flood, the Tower of Babel is only one of thousands throughout the world, why make so much of it? Why invest the Bible's version of mankind's origins with any greater degree of validity than may be found in the Hindu Vedas or any other ancient writings? To answer this common question, we need to fill in a missing piece of the argument offered so far.

The stories in Genesis 1-11 are God's way of reminding men of what they have lost, but for God simply to go on endlessly reminding men that the human race's "real situation," as Lewis says, is estrangement would be uncharacteristic of the God who is Love. With the mythic consciousness of loss and regret, God also gave the hope of restoration. This hope took shape, initially, around an enduring belief in a God who remained constant, worthy of worship; a God unlike the pagan deities, a God whose perfect holiness never faltered, who never debased himself with the vileness readily attributed to the gods of man's inventing. From such a God issued only words of truth, promises of judgment and redemption which we call prophecy.

By common grace, man's universal mythic consciousness perceived faint intimations of a coming hero-redeemer, but these intimations were less than prophecy. Lewis speaks of these mythic clues in this way: "God sent the human race what I call good dreams: I mean those queer stories scattered all through the heathen religions about a god who dies and comes to life again, and by his death, has somehow given new life to men." Lewis is referring to the mythic heroes: Apollo, Hercules, Perseus, Achilles, Dionysus, Adonis, Osiris, Tammuz, Sigurd, Balder, all of whom share some of the characteristics of the redeemer who gives his life to save others. The literature of every nation, including the Hebrew Scriptures, predicts the coming of some such hero.

But the Jewish Scriptures stand apart from the rest because they pass the supreme test. Prophecy is different from mythic intimation because prophecy is inextricably tied to history. Before an event occurs, prophecy must name enough particulars of that event to be veridical. The Jewish Scriptures are prophetic, beginning with Genesis 3:15 and its promise that the Woman's Seed would bruise the Serpent while being bruised by him, and these prophecies are uniquely true.

Only one hero-redeemer appeared in history as the total fulfillment of both myth and prophecy. He was a Jew, Jesus of Nazareth, born of a woman, a descendant of David the King, of the promised seed of Abraham. In every detail of birth, manner of life, death, and miraculous resurrection, the story of Jesus complements the expectations of humanity. Thus the Hebrew Scriptures, the Torah and prophets, rise above other illuminating texts because they point to a holy God revealing himself through a succession of events manifest in history.

Written history and the particular history of the Jewish people have common origins in the development of the Sumerian civilization, from which man's earliest written records have been traced. These records tell of the movement of tribes throughout the valley of the Tigris and Euphrates rivers, along the Fertile Crescent of Mesopotamia. These people founded cities, among them Ur, destroyed by a general flood and afterward rebuilt. Sumerian culture has been studied closely through extensive archaeological findings, which include fragments of business and governmental documents as well as schoolboy exercises dating to before 2500 B. C.

Roughly five centuries later—almost two thousand years before Octavian became *Augustus et Imperator* in Rome—a turning point was reached in the cultural life of the Sumerians. Among one group of Mesopotamians a new sense of tribal identity appears, a racial unity and charter of responsibility founded upon religious faith. This faith impels one man in particular to leave his native peoples and migrate to a new land.

He takes with him a promise that through him and his posterity all nations of the earth would find a blessing.

This man, of course, is Abraham; his departure from Ur is the beginning of Jewish history, documented and authenticated by historical and archaeological research. But it is history closely correlated with myth, for the Lord God who called Abraham, who delivered Lot from Sodom, who revealed himself to Abraham's servant and to Jacob at Bethel, was the same Lord God who, in the transhistorical ages of myth, had punished Adam and Eve, marked Cain, called away Enoch, and commissioned Noah. In calling out the Chaldean Abraham to be his friend, the Lord God was reestablishing his relationship with men, breaking through the veil of myth.

Historically the family of Abraham became the progenitors of David the King and David ben Gurion; of Gideon, judge of Israel, and Gideon Hauser, prosecutor of Nazi criminals; of Saul of Tarsus and Saul Bellow. They called themselves "the chosen people." They were chosen not because of God's arbitrary favor in selecting them and capriciously neglecting the Hittites or Moabites or Egyptians. They were chosen because in the nature of things the hero-redeemer who would rectify the wrong done to men by the first Man in the Garden must himself be a man and must therefore be of one specific ethnic origin. He might have been Eskimo or Chinese. In a wisdom that surpasses human analysis, God determined that the Incarnate Word, the Seed of the Woman, should be a Jew, an Israelite. "They were made God's sons," says St. Paul; "theirs is the splendor of the divine presence, theirs the covenants, the law, the temple worship, and the promises. Theirs are the patriarchs, and from them, in natural descent, sprang the Messiah" (Romans 9:4-5). When this happened, in a crude stable in Bethlehem, *myth* had become *fact.* As C. S. Lewis explains,

> The heart of Christianity is a myth which is also a fact. The old myth of the Dying God, *without ceasing to be myth,* comes down from the heaven of legend and imagination to the earth of history. It *happens*— at a particular date, in a particular place, followed by definable historical consequences. We pass from a Balder or an Osiris, dying nobody knows when or where, to a historical Person crucified (it is all in order) *under Pontius Pilate.*

Now comes the exciting part! Scholars like Joseph Campbell make a great issue of pointing out that "modern scholarship, systematically comparing myths and rites of mankind, has found just about everywhere legends of virgins giving birth to heroes who die and are resurrected." This evidence, we are told, "furnished models to the early Christians for their representation of Christ"—even though any careful reader can tell the difference in character between pagan legends and Christian narratives. The carnal, rapacious gods contrast starkly with the tender power of the Most High overshadowing the Virgin of Nazareth; the young heroes, transmogrified beyond recognition into spring-time flowers, pale against the vigor of the flesh-and-blood Risen Christ. Nevertheless, with this "stunning blow" from scholarship, the Christian believer is expected to stagger in consternation, his faith in the uniqueness of Jesus Christ shattered.

For some it is a shattering experience, especially if they never discover the positive truth that emanates even from pagan distortion. That truth can be found and supported by the doctrine of common grace, as illustrated by C. S. Lewis' apologetics. Lewis takes the findings of scholarship, which are true but which are being used as arrows to attack a higher truth, and turns the weapons back upon their wielders. "The Divine light, we are told, 'lighteneth every man,' " Lewis writes.

> We should, therefore, expect to find in the imagination of great Pagan teachers and myth-makers some glimpse of that theme which we believe to be the very plot of the whole cosmic story—the theme of incarnation, death, and re-birth. And the differences between the Pagan Christs (Balder, Osiris, etc.) and the Christ Himself is much what we should expect to find. . . . It is not the difference between falsehood and truth. It is the difference between a real event on the one hand and dim dreams or premonitions of that same event on the other.

Jesus isn't modeled after Dionysus or any other hero-redeemer. He is the Model from which all prior intimations were taken. In Christ, says St. Paul, "the whole fulness of deity dwells bodily" (Colossians 2:9, RSV). He is the treasured myth of a knowable God become fact in flesh and blood. "So the Word became flesh," the Apostle John says; "he came to dwell among us, and we saw his glory, such glory as befits the Father's only Son, full of grace and truth" (John 1:14).

In myth, observes Walter F. Otto, the word must be the thing itself. So Christians understand the inseparability of God the Father from God the Son and God the Holy Spirit. The Divine Will cannot be divided from the Dynamic Word. The Incarnate Christ is also that Word which, St. John says, "was there from the beginning" (1 John 1:1). Therefore he is the Creative Word which is also the created thing itself, made in his own image, bearing his stamp, breathing the very breath of God, his Spirit.

At the very center of our conception of God-ness are the absolutes of God, qualities already described as Immanent Will, Creative Word, and Supernal Light, which combined in Everlasting Love comprise the Trinity. These absolutes have been codified by theologians into the attributes of God. Through these attributes—God's love and mercy, holiness and justice, omnipresence, omniscience, omnipotence, immutability, and veracity—we come to perceive God's absolutes. But the translation of attributes into absolutes is impossible for human reasoning, working unaided. We cannot understand, for instance, what is meant by "perfect love" or "perfect holiness" because we have never seen or experienced either quality. We have no human point of reference.

The Christian overcomes the inadequacy of his intellect to comprehend the absolutes of God by allowing a spiritual perception within. Often in these terms we speak of the *heart*, as in "I love you with all my *heart*." Through the heart rather than the head we feel an awakening of our dull senses, a quickened illumination. We achieve this spiritual illumination by meditation, prayer, purgation (whether by a literal washing of the body as in baptism or by a figurative cleansing through confession and forgiveness); by song, dance, and our ritualistic participation in the sacrament of bread and wine. When we do these acts, whether alone or in the fellowship of others also initiated into the mystery of the gospel, we are reasserting our relationship, through the Apostles, with Jesus Christ and through Jesus Christ with God. We are able to do this because, as the paleontologist and priest Teilhard de Chardin explains,

> Christ invests himself organically with the very majesty of his creation. And it is in no way metaphorical to say that man finds himself capable of experiencing and discovering his God in the whole length, breadth and depth of the world in movement.

This, too, is what Paul meant when he told the Colossians that Christ

> is the image of the invisible God; his is the primacy over all created things. In him everything in heaven and on earth was created, not only things visible but also the invisible orders of thrones, sovereignties, authorities, and powers: the whole universe has been created

through him and for him. And he exists before everything, and all
things are held together in him. . . . For in him the complete being
of God, by God's own choice, came to dwell. (Colossians 1:15-17, 19)

For the Christian, then, myth is the Word, God's expression
of the inexpressible through Christ, the Christian Reality. Myth
sanctifies man's sense of himself by affirming his everlasting
relationship with God since before the foundations of the earth.
The Christian synthesis of myth and reality frees the believer
from a parochial religion and provides in its place a dynamic
philosophical base from which to see the cosmic order, the surge
of history, and man's place in the scheme of things. The Russian
thinker Nikolai Berdyaev, a declared Christian, saw myth as
"a drama of love and freedom unfolding itself between God
and His other self, which He loves and for whose reciprocal
love He thirsts." But Berdyaev also believed that "only an admission of God's longing for His other self can provide a solution
of celestial history and, through it, of the destinies of both man
and the world."

Thus the significance of the Bible is its written record of God's
admission to men that, having created a being in image and
likeness to himself, God is incomplete until restored in love to
the lost creature. Yet the very baldness of these words—the
audacity that anyone should speak of God as *incomplete*—
exceeds our comprehending. As the Psalmist said, "Such knowledge is beyond my understanding, so high that I cannot reach
it" (Psalm 139:6).

* * *

Does all this mean, someone may ask, that the Bible is "full of
myths," as the popular misstatement puts it? Of course not.
It does mean that when we try to speak to God or about
God, we often find that speech turns to "inarticulate groans,"
as St. Paul said (Romans 8:26). Or we find the writer resorting
to what Martin Luther described as "things truly accomplished,
but poetically handled." Thereby the writer attempts to corre-
late the *word* with the *thing being said*, to give substance to the
truth he has been shown.

At a superficial level there may seem to be value in broaden-
ing the view of divine revelation to include all myth and
mythologies equally. Surely—some would say—the Bible reveals
enough of the character of God to make us see parallels
between a polytheistic mythology and a monotheistic faith.

Why, then, may not the Greek and Roman conceptions of divine attributes—as well as the mythologies of any culture—be identified by the Christian and cherished as oblique representations of an absolute God in all his wholeness? Isn't there room in Christian myth for the mythology of other religions?

This was precisely the question to which St. Paul addressed himself when, standing on the Areopagus, the hill named for Ares or Mars, he told the Athenians,

> Men of Athens, I see that in everything that concerns religion you are uncommonly scrupulous. For as I was going around looking at the objects of your worship, I noticed among other things an altar bearing the inscription "To an Unknown God." What you worship but do not know—this is what I now proclaim. (Acts 17:22-23)

To Romans who had already claimed faith in Christ, Paul wrote of the consequences of trusting in a devious mythology, rather than in the revealed truth of God. Pagan idolaters, he said, "boast of their wisdom, but they have made fools of themselves, exchanging the splendor of immortal God for an image shaped like mortal man, even for images like birds, beasts, and creeping things" (Romans 1:22-23).

Christianity isn't a religion of myths or mythology. Paul instructed his protégé Timothy to forbid certain persons from "teaching erroneous doctrines and studying those interminable myths and genealogies, which issue in mere speculation and cannot make known God's plan for us, which works through faith" (1 Timothy 1:3-4). Likewise Paul wrote to Titus to warn him against the Cretan tendency toward lazy thinking, in particular telling him to beware of "Jewish myths and commandments of merely human origin, the work of men who turn their backs upon the truth" (Titus 1:14).

The Apostle Peter rebutted any argument intended to suggest that the New Way of faith in a resurrected Christ was merely its own collection of myths and fairy tales. Relying upon the indisputable authority of personal experience, he wrote, "For we did not follow cleverly devised myths when we made known to you the power and coming of our Lord Jesus Christ, but we were eyewitnesses of his majesty" (2 Peter 1:16, RSV).

Yet Christian doctrine begins in the hidden world of mythic consciousness, illumined only by the Eternal Light, communicated by the Eternal Word. To this reservoir of cosmic scope the artist comes to fill his imagination.

CHAPTER FOUR

a sanctified imagination

The Word creates, sustains creation, and liberates his creatures enslaved by the tyranny of falseness. The Word liberates through his sovereignty as the One in whom "all things are held together" (Colossians 1:17). But according to the divine program, the Word also calls upon men to share the mystery of the gospel with others.

The first proclaimers of the mystery were the poets and seers who sang the story later transcribed to written form as the opening chapters of Genesis. They weren't public officials, scribes, or correspondents, such as later wrote the chronicles of Israel's kings or took down the messages from the mouths of Israel's prophets. These were men to whom had been entrusted a particular gift of poetic expression, a gift of sanctified imagination to dramatize the phenomena of human experience intersected by the presence of a personal God. Acting under the impulse of the Trinity—the Will, the Light, the Word—they recounted a truthful vision of the world's beginnings, Man's earliest state, and the cataclysmic consequences of sin.

These myth-tellers weren't making it up as they went along. Theirs was no improvisational vision, "for it was not through any human whim," St. Peter avers, "that men prophesied of old; men they were, but, compelled by the Holy Spirit, they spoke the words of God" (2 Peter 1:21).

Perhaps to some, Peter's description of divine inspiration still evokes a human stenographer taking dictation from the Big Boss. The Bible itself disallows any such distortion, for it offers not one authorized biography of Jesus but four distinctly different and fragmentary life-narratives. Here and there in the Old Testament we find the same event recorded twice and from slightly different human perspectives. But the divine perspective remains constant. The process of inspiration cannot violate the methods of the Trinity in Creation. God the Eternal Will stimulates the writer; God the Eternal Light clarifies the mystery; God the Eternal Word provides the means of expression. But at this same moment the divine provision for human individuality, human uniqueness, takes over so that every man expresses praise in his own tongue, every man according to his own sanctified imagination, transfiguring mundanity into sublimity.

Inspiration means that a conscious mind, operating under the influence of God, inscribed the truth of God. But before the truth of God spoke from the page in words, it had existed in myth; before its revelation in myth, it had preexisted as the Word. Only an imagination steeped in holy possibilities could be receptive enough to absorb and transmit the truth of the Word through myth to language. A sanctified imagination is such a mind, committed to the fundamental truth being revealed and recognizing that its source lies in the verity of God himself.

In Genesis 1-11 we have a clear instance of a conscious mind using figurative and poetic language to tell the truth in a mythic mode, by means of his sanctified imagination. However, in suggesting that Genesis 1-11 be read as sacred myth, I allow no inference to be drawn that the text is either false or unhistorical. It is both true and historical. It is true that the Almighty and Triune God created the world out of nothing. It is historical as no other event has ever been, for it is the first act of history that coincides time with eternity. These chapters are also historical in another sense because, as the editors of *The Jerusalem Bible* say,

> they declare the fundamental truths on which the plan of salvation rests. These truths are: the Creation by God at the beginning of time, God's special intervention in the making of man and woman, the unity of the human race, the sin of our first parents, the fall from divine favor and the penalties their descendants would inherit in consequence of the sin. All these are truths which have their bearing on theological doctrine and which are guaranteed by the authority of scripture; but they are also facts, and the certainty of the truths implies the reality of the facts. It is in this sense that the first chapters of Genesis are called historical.

The novelist John Fowles has written, "Genesis is a great lie; but it is also a great poem." This glib incongruity expresses a common misunderstanding of the relationship between infinite truth and the finite means of expression. Genesis is true, Genesis is historical; but it is not eye-witness history such as we have elsewhere in literature, including other parts of the Bible. It is the retelling of a story from far in the past, such a far distant past that no one can comment on the exactness of any of its details, since no one living at the time Genesis was written was present at the Creation—except the God who willed, enlightened, and gave expression to the scribe responsible for the text.

We can pause for a moment to ask, Who was that scribe and what was his role in putting together the text? Tradition has generally attributed the entire Pentateuch—Genesis through Deuteronomy—to Moses, even though Moses' own death is recorded in Deuteronomy 34, making his authorship of at least that chapter doubtful. Many critics reject a Mosaic authorship, but even for the sake of argument granting it to Moses, it is unreasonable to suppose that none of the patriarchs who preceded Moses had ever questioned their antecedents, that none had ever known the reasons for honoring the Lord God as supreme.

Whoever the scribe was or however many there may have been, the stories in Genesis 1-11 represent the ancient custom of oral transfer of tribal beliefs from fathers to sons, from generation to generation. Anthropologists know even today that among primitive peoples the ceremonial telling of tribal lore is part of youth's rites of passage into manhood. Around the fire, around the altar, at some appointed time and place, the elders relate stories taught them by their fathers; the young learn to repeat the stories as told.

Evidence of the custom appears in Genesis 4:23-24, where Lamech, a descendant of Cain and like Cain a murderer, boasts of his exploits to his wives.

> I kill a man for wounding me,
> a young man for a blow.

Lamech's song continues with a direct reference to the Lord's promise of sevenfold vengeance upon anyone who kills Cain. The tradition, carried by word of mouth throughout Cain's posterity, gives Lamech sanction for his precipitate action.

The author or authors of Genesis carried the Hebrew myth of Creation and the Fall from its oral form into writing. But they didn't change its oracular nature. The myth remains in all its majesty. It is not a technical treatise explaining precisely *how* God created the world; it tells only that God did so. Then the author supplies the implications that follow, implications affecting himself and his reader. Because God made the world and because the world turned away from him, moral disaster accompanied by physical death followed. This is the message the proclaimer of myth must tell.

Furthermore, because of who the writer is—a Jew conscious of his heritage as one of Abraham's seed—he must do more than merely retell an ancient story about Creation. He must also communicate a lasting and immediate truth. That truth leads him beyond the details of his story to see the role of his people, the people of Israel, as the chosen of God. He knows that from these people will come a hero who will restore the lost order to the world. How this will happen the writer of Genesis 1-11 does not explain, except to make plain that the expected hero-redeemer will be human like the Woman, vulnerable yet ultimately victorious over the monstrous evil. It isn't the writer's obligation to tell more than this; his obligation is to show his readers how Man, created in the image and likeness of God, came to need such a hero to restore him in fellowship to his Creator.

But how is it written down? What makes it *mythic*? In Chapter 1, for instance, the language is primarily figurative, as it must be, if only because the human mind has no possible way by which to give ideas of formlessness upon which the initial description of chaos depends. In going back to the very beginning of beginnings, a thoroughly paradoxical problem faces the writer: He must try to tell what the world was like before it was *like* anything! "The truth of creation," wrote Reinhold Niebuhr, "can be expressed only in terms which outrage reason." The writer must therefore resort to an imaginative representation of what he can't even begin to express in literal terms.

Carl Jung finds nothing extraordinary about the human writer's appeal to myth "to give his experience its most fitting expression." But, Jung continues,

> it would be a serious mistake to suppose that he works with materials received at secondhand. The primordial experience is the source of his creativeness; it cannot be fathomed, and therefore requires mythological imagery to give it form. In itself it offers no words or images, for it is a vision seen "as in a glass, darkly." It is merely a deep presentiment that strives to find expression.... Since

the particular expression can never exhaust the possibilities of the vision, but falls far short of it in richness of content, the poet must have at his disposal a huge store of materials if he is to communicate even a few of his intimations.

Throughout Genesis 1-11, to which we now turn, the writer develops the epic of mankind's origins around a series of actions involving mythic implications, growing out of the intimations of his sanctified imagination.

* * *

The creative energy that brought the world into being also inspired certain men to tell its wonders. Their vehicle was language conveying its mythic message in a poetic manner—that is to say, figuratively rather than literally; by means of symbol and verisimilitude, by compression and metaphor. The form these words assume reminds us of a great poem, as John Fowles has said, constructed on the grandest possible scale, demanding the broadest scope.

Herman Melville was right: "To write a mighty book, you must have a mighty theme." The mighty theme in Genesis 1-11 is the cosmic movement from order to chaos, repeated over and over. It appears first by inference in Genesis 1:1, "In the beginning God created the heavens and the earth" (RSV). A high view of God's creatorship prevents us from assuming that his original handiwork, his *poem*, was in chaos and ruin. Yet in verse 2, we read of formlessness, void, and darkness. Either the writer is developing the act of Creation in slow stages, including as he goes along the early shapelessness one might observe in a sculptor's workshop; or else something happened to alter the original conditions of order, at least on this planet. If something did indeed occur, this writer does not choose to explain; from later evidence, however, may we not infer the rebellion of Satan causing, in Gerard Manley Hopkins' phrase, "the bent World"?

In any case, in verse 3 order comes through the summoning of Light, not to be confused with celestial lights. The poet James Weldon Johnson imagines that

> Then God smiled,
> And the light broke,
> And the darkness rolled up on one side,
> And the light stood shining on the other,
> And God said, *"That's good!"*

From this point Creation proceeds, until God's summary estimate, that everything he had made was "very good."

As if in consummate evidence of good order, God ordained the Sabbath as a day of rest—a luxury available to those whose work is done but a necessity for those whose sense of continuing labor recognizes the need for rest. The Sabbath is both a day to worship the Creator and a time for relaxation from the mental and physical stress of labor. "The Sabbath was made for the sake of man," Jesus reminded the legalists of his day, "and not man for the Sabbath" (Mark 2:27). In so saying he confirmed the religious, psychological, and physiological warrants for combining meditation with recreation, thereby liberating spirit, mind, and body.

The first story, the first phase of the Creation myth, concludes on a note of satisfaction and the contemplation of God's finished work. His climactic act in the series of creative events has been the making of Man to care for all the rest of nature, another evidence of God's concern for order. This theme continues and dominates Chapter 2, with a slightly altered perspective to the telling. Whereas the creating, energizing elements of Chapter 1 were fire and air—light and wind—the writer in Chapter 2 uses water and earth. In Chapter 1, Man is a mostly spiritual being, made in the image and likeness of God who is Spirit; in Chapter 2, Man is "a living creature" with physical needs—a home, an adequate food supply, refreshing rivers, companionship—and certain clear limitations not imposed on pure spirit.

The writer of Chapter 2 informs us of the first prohibition, forbidding Man from eating the fruit of the tree of the knowledge of good and evil. The command is stern and threatening, although limited only to the one tree. The tree of life isn't even mentioned, as though both the myth-teller and his audience assume that not even naive Man in his infant state would need to be told not to usurp that prerogative.

Not quite in the nature of a command but nonetheless another evidence of God's concern for order is the search for Man's most suitable companion. Men and women belong together for several reasons. Sexual reproduction after their kind is one reason and adequately exposes any desire for homosexuality or bestiality as essentially a form of genocide, since either perversion fails to reproduce men in the image of God. But there are other reasons also. The writer's proof that Woman was meant to be Man's partner is that they communicate with each other in language. Man could name the animals but not speak with them. They weren't his partners because they didn't share with him what he shared with God, the capacity to speak.

With the introduction of disobedience and sin in Chapter 3, chaos again returns to disrupt the order of God's creation. The nakedness that symbolizes the innocence of Adam and Eve at the end of Chapter 2 becomes the first sign of self-condemnation. But even though God's divine retribution falls upon the disobeying Man and Woman to bring an end to anarchy, the fact that corruption has entered Man's experience cannot be erased. The remaining chapters of this section continue the same rhythmic pattern, order-to-chaos-to-order-to-chaos.

But a great myth may be interpreted at more than one level; just so, the first eleven chapters of Genesis treat more than the single theme of order and chaos. Here too is the theme of God's search for fulfillment in Man, as well as of Man's need for companionship both with God and with fellow human beings. From the outset the Bible makes it clear that God isn't an impersonal deity: he cares for his creatures; he expects his creatures to care for each other—man to care for woman, brother to care for brother. In the creation of Man; in the creation of Woman to be Man's companion; in the lonely, poignant question to Adam, "Where are you?" (Genesis 3:9); in the comparable question to Cain, "Where is your brother Abel?" (Genesis 4:9); in his searching out a means of propagating the race while destroying its evil influences; in the promise of the rainbow—in all these acts and signs, God makes known his concern for mankind.

The broken relationship occurs in Chapter 3, perhaps the most important narrative in the Old Testament. Here the participants, the objects, the actions, are most evocative of symbolic interpretation; indeed, each represents more than its own literal value. But the *dramatis personae* of Genesis 3 are more than characters in a play, more than archetypes from Jung's "collective unconscious" or from the sanctified imagination of the Jewish writer. They lay the very foundation on which the Christian gospel rests. Without Genesis 3, there would be no counterbalancing account such as John 19 and 20. I'm not arguing here for what is sometimes called the theory of a "fortunate Fall"—Aren't we happy that Adam sinned because if he hadn't, we would never have known the love of Jesus!—but I'm saying that the whole story of redemption requires all its parts, including the reason mankind needs to be redeemed.

The participants in Chapter 3 are the Man and Woman, the Serpent, and the Lord God. The location is the paradise garden; the objects are two trees, the fruit of one, leaves from a third, the skins of animals, and the cherubim's flaming sword.

The Man and Woman serve both the myth and history in dual roles. As mythic characters they represent the cause for that primal sense of loss—what Melville called "the sum of all the general rage and hate felt by his whole race from Adam down." From the mythic view the Man and Woman transcend any mere identification as Adam and Eve. But as human beings, upon whom rested the first responsibility for biological reproduction after their kind, they are finite. Blessed with special privileges, they are nonetheless restricted as all human beings must be by that discipline which alone makes freedom possible.

Their home is Eden, belonging to no particular geography but set in the East of the writer's inspired imagination. It is a fertile park producing "ambrosial fruit / Of vegetable gold"—a veritable Garden of the Hesperides, as Milton suggests. Gerard Manley Hopkins sees a perfect spring day as reminiscent of

> A strain of the earth's sweet being in the beginning
> In Eden garden.

As God had created Man in his own image, so God created Man's home in likeness to the heavenly home. According to the description in the Book of the Revelation, the holy city is a bejewelled park where flows the river of life, where stands the tree of life.

In Eden, however, God adds another tree not found in Heaven, the tree of the knowledge of good and evil. The very accessibility of this tree and its fruit points to Man's free will. "Paradise is of the option," wrote Emily Dickinson. God permitted Man the power of choice: obedience or disobedience, innocence or the terrifying knowledge of right and wrong with its accompanying obligation to choose.

The decision to disobey is made at the urging of the Serpent. The writer of Genesis never identifies the Serpent, except to place him in a category different from any other creature God had made. One must return to John's Revelation to find the explicit statement, "that serpent of old, the Devil or Satan"

(Revelation 20:2). But the writer leaves no doubt of the Serpent's allegiance: He is contrary to God, he is committed to the pride of self-importance. Furthermore, the use of a Serpent-figure as the manifestation of evil corresponds to a common understanding in many parts of the world, that the snake is a symbol of paramount evil. Here is clearly an instance of the all-pervasive nature of myth. While the Bible mentions very few of the monstrous creatures who frightened ancient peoples—Behemoth and Leviathan in the Book of Job and the dragon Rahab in Isaiah 51:9 are exceptions—there is no mistaking the common recognition of the Serpent and who he represents.

The Serpent also tempts through his appeal to the senses, and in the face of his argument God's forbidding seems little more than the petty demand of a spoilsport. It's worth noting that the fruit is *taboo*, banned by sacred interdiction, another common mythic trait. Appropriately, the act of disobedience and its guilty consequences derive from a violation of the taboo against eating the fruit. Of course God's order could have been anything—not to cross a certain stream, not to touch a certain rock, or (as in the story of Eros and Psyche) not to attempt to look directly at his face. But the author of Genesis, inspired to exercise his sanctified imagination, develops in token of disobedience the ingestion of food and nakedness in token of guilt.

In Genesis the act of disobedience is deliberate rebellion; it is sin. The Man and Woman don't stumble by accident into God's disfavor; they pause to consider, then eat. They fondle the fruit and find it "pleasing to the eye and tempting to contemplate" (Genesis 3:6). They take into their physical systems the corruption of disobedience. Their sin is enough, in time, to snuff out the breath of life.

Their immediate reaction is the bitter fulfillment of part of the Serpent's promise, "Your eyes will be opened and you will be like gods knowing both good and evil" (Genesis 3:5). Indeed, their eyes were opened, but instead of perceiving *both* good and evil, they recognize only evil and experience only shame. The exact nature of their shame is something more than nakedness, just as the exact nature of the fruit was something more than juice and pulp. That fruit was *knowledge*. When it

was eaten, the Man and Woman knew what they had not
known before.

God had made them naked and pronounced them beautiful;
in perfect innocence they had delighted in each other and their
differences. Their union, the two becoming one flesh, had been
like the Trinity in its blending of will and word lighted by the
warmth of love. Now in the aftermath of sin, love is merely
sex and sex turns to shame. The union dissolves into a separate
study of their bodies, like curious children in a barnyard. No
longer innocent, contaminated as they are by pride, their curi-
osity becomes cause for self-gratification, for withholding oneself from the other, for shame. They are confounded and dismayed by a terrible new knowledge—the knowledge that love
means giving and lust means taking. Their flimsy fig-leaf cover-
ings represent mankind's first inadequate attempt to hide from
each other. As a result of the Fall, nakedness becomes "indecent
exposure," and sexual intercourse, even in sophisticated America, often hides itself in a darkened room with partners nearly
fully clothed.

The next step is to hide from God behind the trees of Eden,
but when this fails they try to hide behind each other's blame,
and the union degenerates into alibi and accusation.

God's presence in the garden is signified by "the evening
breeze," another manifestation of the Spirit, like "the mighty
wind" in Chapter 1. But the mighty God comes in gentleness to
greet his creatures, like a zephyr rustling the leaves of trees
behind which hide the Man and Woman. The writer uses
anthropomorphic language to describe God's "walking in the
garden" (Genesis 3:8). The point is not whether God who is
Spirit has legs; the point is the *presence* of God, his daily renewal
of his relationship with Man.

The interrogation which God puts the Man and Woman
through isn't necessary for his sake; clearly the writer of Genesis
believes in an omniscient deity. But it's essential for Man, to dis-
close the depths to which he has fallen. The love-song of Chapter 2 turns to ashes in the mouth as Adam indicts Eve—and
with his indictment blames God for having given her as a companion in the first place! The Woman knows she has been
deceived, but her reply is the petulance of a seduced woman
unwilling to admit her willingness to submit. Only the Serpent remains silent.

God's judgment matches Man's disobedience; the punishment fits the crime. But it also fulfills one of the secondary purposes of the ancient writer, to explain the phenomena of life as he has observed them. He chooses, in Genesis 3, to explain three sepa- rate aspects of natural phenomena:

1. why snakes crawl on their bellies;
2. why women suffer labor pangs in childbirth;
3. why men must work hard to earn their living.

A spiritual phenomenon is also explained, although only infer- entially. When Man sins he must pay the consequences, as we have seen. But paying the consequences doesn't atone for the sin. Man can't cover up his imperfections. God alone provides the adequate covering, but to do so requires the suffering and sacrifice of a third party—in this case, the animals whose skins became tunics for Adam and Eve.

The chapter concludes with the writer's introduction of the final and principal theme, the fact of Man's subsequent aliena- tion from God. In his present lapsed condition, Man is unfit for the near presence of God. If he should now extend his boldness to reach out and take the fruit of the tree of life, he would live forever but in the same fallen state, like his tempter Satan. To be kept from that fate, Man must die and be reborn, this time as a being fully eligible to taste the eternal tree of life. All this will come to pass, the writer is certain, with the appearance of the Woman's child, the hero-redeemer. Mean- time, in Milton's magnificent vision of paradise lost, the Man and Woman

> . . . hand in hand, with wandering steps and slow,
> Through Eden took their solitary way.

At the barred eastern gate stand the cherubim wielding flam- ing swords. But the truth is plain that for Man there is no way back to the innocence he knew before the Fall; no way to regain the relationship lost with God; no way past the gates to the tree of life—until the Third Party provides the garments of atone- ment. That day is promised in Revelation 22:14: "Happy are those who wash their robes clean! They will have the right to the tree of life and will enter by the gates of the city."

*   *   *

The tone of this analysis intends to suggest not only the fullness of imagination present in the Bible's account of the

Beginning, but also the seriousness with which it ought to be read. Of course some will think this approach wrongheaded. Those who see myth as something primitive, outmoded, technologically unsound, leading rather to intellectual disarray than to art and truth, will perhaps agree with J. H. Plumb. He speaks of myth as "the specious sophistries by which we permit ourselves to accept evil, suffering, subjection." He complains, "We are still dominated by mythical explanations of the universe; myth still haunts social and sexual customs."

But can we, as Plumb and others argue we must, rid ourselves of myth? Can we, merely by taking thought, root out of our consciousness the story of Adam's Fall? Can we choke off the resonant responses evoked from the depths of our being? Would we indeed be better painters and writers, better husbands and fathers—better persons—if we did so? Stanley Burnshaw provides an answer when he writes,

> To break through the seamless web—no longer to be part of all that one senses and knows—is to enter a strangeness from which there is no return. Paradigms of the fate can be found in ancient myths which compress to a single moment long ages during which men slowly came to realize what they had "done" and lost. If the drama of Eden is much more explicit about disobedience-punishment-pain than about sin, no one can doubt that the latter stands for the sense of loss, uneasiness, and fear that accuses a creature outside the paradise-web. . . . The tales of the race's childhood are songs of paradise lost, of homelessness, helplessness: the lament of a creature aware of his alienation from the whole of living creation.

In the mythic fact of Eden, man's daily experience of separation, incompleteness, frustration and irretrievable loss is given its original source.

"There is no natural phenomenon and no phenomenon of human life," wrote Ernst Cassirer, "that is not capable of a mythical interpretation, and which does not call for such an interpretation." As if in response to that statement, one comes upon this poem by Dickinson:

> Eden is that old-fashioned House
> We dwell in every day
> Without suspecting our abode
> Until we drive away.
>
> How fair on looking back, the Day
> We sauntered from the Door—
> Unconscious our returning,
> But discover it no more.

No, Plumb is deluded if he thinks it's possible for man to live without a recollection of his past, no matter how embarrassingly that recollection condemns his conduct. Skeptics who would root out the mythic consciousness would, by so doing, eliminate man's sense of who he is and why; they would also extirpate the hope man holds for becoming something better.

This hope is what motivates the Christian imagination. Myth is more than "specious sophistries." It finds its historical verification in the lives of men from Abraham to the present. If there was a Serpent entwined around the tree of knowledge whose presence meant death, there was also a serpent coiled around the healing staff of Aesculapius and a brazen serpent on a pole in the wilderness. From these intimations the Christian knows what Jesus meant when he told Nicodemus, "This Son of Man must be lifted up as the serpent was lifted up by Moses in the wilderness, so that everyone who has faith in him may in him possess eternal life" (John 3:14).

The Christian imagination can't afford to dismiss the stories of Heracles and Jason, of Hippomenes and Orion, of Theseus and Perseus, of Sisyphus and Tantalus, to mention only a few Greek names. The Bible itself speaks of such men, a race of giants, demigods, and superheroes who inhabited the earth between the Fall and the Flood: "In those days, when the sons of the gods had intercourse with the daughters of men and got children by them, the Nephilim were on earth. They were the heroes of old, men of renown" (Genesis 6:4).

As for the Flood itself, every Near Eastern culture had its own story comparable to the Genesis account of a worldwide deluge. Anthropologists have uncovered scores of similar stories in other parts of the world, including Formosa, Southeast Asia, and Malaysia. The Greeks told of Deucalion and Pyrrha, son and niece of Prometheus, whose piety saved them when Zeus decided to destroy the world by flood. Prometheus had warned Deucalion and told him to build a wooden chest in which to hide. When the rains came, they were safely within the chest, which floated to the top of Mount Parnassus. When the waters receded, this sole surviving pair emerged and gave thanks.

The Sumerians knew a similar story, of a man named Ziusudra; the Babylonians called him Utnapishtim; the Hebrews, of course, Noah. Beyond these minor differences in names lies a common significance far more important than contemporary studies in geological data or even the supposed discovery of a ship's hull imbedded in a glacier on Ararat! At the heart of the universal flood story lies the truth of God's abiding revelation of himself and its preservation through the common grace of myth.

What Jung calls "the collective unconscious" is, for the Christian, that remaining perception among all men of the "light which enlightens every man," the light of God's truth, the disclosure of God's invisible attributes. Because of the Fall and Man's estrangement from God, mankind toils in almost total darkness. But in the midnight of his lostness, even there, the light of memory and the hope of restoration shine on in men's response to myth.

The Christian writer's imagination must be sparked to show the reality of myth in terms that suit his own times. This doesn't mean that the writer needs to invent "new" myths. His effort would be futile, for there are no new myths; there are only reenactments of the old. The man at work on a secret project under abandoned football bleachers was Enrico Fermi; he might have been Prometheus. The test pilot aloft over Edwards Air Force Base, is he not also Icarus? Could not John Keats have been describing Neil Armstrong's lift-off from Tranquility Base as readily as Endymion's farewell to the Moon?

> . . . when like taper-flame
> Left sudden by a dallying breath of air,
> He rose In silence, and once more 'gan fare
> Along his fated way.

Many modern men and women can look back to a time in their recent past when a subtle tempter convinced them that with only a taste of this or that their eyes would be opened and they would be like gods. How many of these same men and women know that they have lost what they can never regain and, like the boy Ralph at the end of William Golding's *Lord of the Flies*, find themselves weeping for the end of Innocence? How many brothers lie crumpled at our feet while we go about our business, asking our cynical questions about who's responsible? How many towers must we build—skyscrapers of futility— before we realize that the babel of tongues cannot be translated simultaneously, that the ideal of world peace received its first crushing veto with Cain's jealous rage?

In his trilogy of interplanetary novels—*Out of the Silent*

Planet, Perelandra, and *That Hideous Strength*—C. S. Lewis has used some of these themes from classical and biblical myth as a framework for his narratives. *Perelandra* makes an interesting example. A philology professor from Cambridge named Elwin Ransom is taken to Perelandra, the planet Venus. There he sees the embodiment of personages known to him as Ares and Aphrodite, the patrons of the planets Mars and Venus. He speaks with them and learns that Earth has been cut off from the rest of the universe by the rebellion of Lucifer, who has made our planet his stronghold. As a result, stories of the relationships between God and his creatures have filtered to Earthlings through many distortions. Ransom thinks to himself,

> Our mythology is based on a solider reality than we dream; but it is also at an almost infinite distance from that base. And when they told him this, Ransom at last understood why mythology was what it was—gleams of celestial strength and beauty falling on a jungle of filth and imbecility. His cheeks burned on behalf of our race when he looked on the true Mars and Venus and remembered the follies that have been talked of them on Earth.

Ransom also meets the king and queen of Perelandra and an old antagonist, a scientist named Weston. Through Weston, he discovers, Satan is trying to infect Perelandra for the first time. Weston attempts to lure the queen into disobeying God—the parallels with Genesis 3 are obvious! But Ransom also discovers why he is on Perelandra: to contend against Weston and save the queen from disobeying. His struggle with Weston is at first only argument, then violence, from which Ransom receives a wound in his heel. But in the end the queen resists temptation, and there is no second Fall.

The God over history never repeats himself. Instead he specializes in providing singular revelations of his power—one Creation, one Flood, one Chosen People, one Redeemer, one Resurrection, and therefore one Book whose writers could affirm that what they said, God said. This historical uniqueness marks the Bible; a special providence preserves its integrity. But the divine interplay of forces responsible for Creation and for the telling of Creation's story also provides illumination for writers throughout history. I don't mean that Dante, Milton, and T. S. Eliot experienced in kind or degree the same power of inspiration that motivated and enlightened Isaiah and Paul, for the historical reason just cited. I do mean that writers since Hermas

wrote his *Shepherd* early in the second century after Christ
have been gifted with a sanctified imagination.

God who is Light, said St. Paul, "has caused his light to shine
within us, to give the light of revelation—the revelation of the
glory of God in the face of Jesus Christ" (2 Corinthians 4:6).
Gazing at that revelation through faith, the Christian writer
sees in Christ the brightness of his glory, the express image of
God's resplendent being. In Dorothy Sayers' terms, Christ is
the Image of the Unimaginable, and "in the depths of their
mysterious being, the Unimaginable and the Image are *one and
the same.*"

But the writer knows he can't conduct such radiance directly;
it must be represented, as Dickinson says, "slant . . . in circuit"—
by metaphor and by myth. And so through the rhetoric of his
sanctified imagination the writer reshapes his vision of Christ
into a shining story of grace.

CHAPTER FIVE

the rhetoric of the gospel

On the south side of Washington Square Park in New York City stands the Adoniram Judson Memorial Church, named for the pioneer Baptist missionary to Burma. In recent years the church has become notorious as a base for experimental modes of worship, including bizarre drama or nude dancing in the chancel.

The passerby receives eloquent testimony of this church's sense of mission from its cornerstone. Extruding from the foundation is a fountain in hexagonal shape. On its several faces, in faded carving, one may still read "Let him that is athirst come and drink of the water of life freely." At one time, I suppose, the drinking fountain operated for all to use. But in the twenty-five years that I have known Judson Memorial Church, I have never seen the fountain in working condition. I have seen it closed by a metal cover, padlocked and splattered with city filth; I have seen it shut off from common access by a spear-like iron fence. In other words, the invitation of the fountain's inscription is meaningless.

Contradictions like this no longer surprise us. We have grown accustomed to disparities between what is said and what is done, conflicts between language and life, between the word and the thing itself. In the loose and often inaccurate parlance of our society, such discrepancies are often blamed on *rhetoric*— "mere rhetoric." The word becomes a pejorative in phrases like "political rhetoric" or "the rhetoric of Madison Avenue." We think of rhetoric in connection with Polonius.

But this is a distortion of the word. Rhetoric is and has been for centuries an honorable art, the art of arranging language through the use of various patterns and options to achieve the most effective communication. In Greece and Rome the study of rhetoric was part of classical education. Some of the world's wisest men have been teachers of rhetoric: Aristotle, Cicero, and Augustine, for example, all formulated important statements on rhetoric. St. Paul no doubt studied rhetoric, perhaps at school in Tarsus or under Gamaliel; he was a skilled Christian rhetorician, both as speaker and writer.

One ancient rhetorician proposed that a man's choice of rhetoric might reveal something about his character, that a man might be known by the very words he uses and how he arranges them and to what purpose. This concept was later expressed by Comte de Buffon, who said, "The style is the man." In our own time, the American essayist and novelist E. B. White has said much the same thing: "Style *is* the writer, and therefore what a man is, rather than what he knows, will at last determine his style." And no less an authority on human nature than Jesus Christ said, "For the words that the mouth utters come from the overflowing of the heart" (Luke 6:45).

These characterizations of rhetoric extend well beyond the limits of the printed page; they merge with the behavior of the rhetorician. The King James Version of the Bible translates *anastrophe,* the Greek word for "deportment" or "manner of living," as "conversation." There is a subtle relationship to be maintained between "conversation" and the idea that a man's rhetoric mirrors his character.

If this is so, what does the rhetoric of today tell us about ourselves? What will it reveal to historians in the future—supposing that we do not destroy ourselves and the future with us! The philosopher William Barrett suggests that "a painful irony" is apparent to anyone who considers, on the one hand, the sophistication of our technology and, on the other hand, the inner poverty exposed through our art. Barrett says,

> What cannot man do! He has greater power now than Prometheus or Icarus or any of those daring mythical heroes who were later to succumb to the disaster of pride. But if an observer from Mars were to turn his attention from these external appurtenances of power to the shape of man as revealed in our novels, plays, painting, and sculpture, he would find there a creature full of holes and gaps, faceless, riddled with doubts and negations, starkly finite.

Yet this is not the message we receive from most social commentators. We hear instead of the glory of our new freedoms and the wonder of our passage into the Age of Aquarius. We are congratulated on having emerged from the prissiness of Clark Gable's "Damn!" in *Gone with the Wind* to twelve-letter obscenities on a New York stage. This, we are to suppose, is what it means for man to have come of age: He can now be shameless about admitting an incestuous lust for his mother.

One could look, as Barrett says, at any number of novels, films, plays, musicals, paintings, and other offerings to obtain a sense of the rhetoric, the conduct of life, that speaks for our time. As an example, *Hair*, the "American Tribal-Love Rock Musical" whose four-year run on Broadway closed in 1972, presents itself as a prototype of American life, anarchistic and improvisational. In fact, however, the show was a contradiction of its own aims. Instead of being radical in its form, *Hair* was carefully structured and contrived. Its gestures were studied, its music commercial; its lyrics combined modish audacity with clichés and bromides reminiscent of Nellie Forbush and Lieutenant Joe Cable in *South Pacific*. *Hair* was more a dramatized concert than a music drama; the performers were singers, not actors. Its best moment may have been the famous nude scene that closed the first act with

> Where do I go?
> And will I ever discover why I live and die?

The nudity, for all its original sensationalism, contributed to the song's sense of futility and essential aloneness. It came as one of the most restrained moments in the play; it may have been, in fact, the most chaste as well. For *Hair*, if the truth be told, was an interminable dirty joke—not funny, not ribald, not bawdy in the manner of great comedy—but dirty in the puerile and crude fashion of the junior high school locker room or the lavatory in a bus depot.

The song "Sodomy" places *Hair* in its philosophical context. After enumerating several varieties of sexual perversion, the singer concludes that "masturbation can be fun." This declaration typifies the level of serious thought arrived at in the play; it also characterizes the mode of life, the *conversation*, the rhetoric of *Hair*'s constituents. It points unmistakably to the early-adolescent mentality in its preoccupation with pubic hair and the developing human body. Hence the repeated gesturing, the imitations of sexual intercourse, the self-conscious autoeroticism, all manifestly isolated, alienated, cut off from any possible experience of joy—just as masturbation must be. The closing song, "Let the Sunshine In," must be one of the most ironic and anticlimactic finales in the history of musical theatre.

Yet this show claims to speak the truth, to speak for America. For years its principal advertisement read: "Discover America. See *Hair!*" What is its message? Like other productions of its kind, *Hair* reverberated with falsity, maintaining that chaos is freedom (while hypocritically repeating the same lines, the same blocking night after night); that discord is harmony (while singing and playing rhyming words set to conventional chord structures). It maintained that violence is an acceptable form of natural expression (while protesting an overseas war). Nowhere in *Hair* could one learn that psychosis or neurosis is more than a novelty to be exposed to public ridicule or that hypersexuality is also common among dog-packs chasing a bitch in heat. Instead one felt that the young people performing in this show had never been told that all their shocking language had been said before, by Marine drill instructors and by little boys trying to sound tough.

"The words that the mouth utters come from the overflowing of the heart," Jesus said, and so we shouldn't be surprised at the rhetoric of the ungodly. America, like Israel in the days of Isaiah, is "a people of unclean lips" (Isaiah 6:5). Like Isaiah, we need to have our mouths cleansed, not with the soap-and-water of religious practice, not with the flavored mouthwash of good deeds, but by the fire of God's holiness.

In the mouths of some professed prophets—secular theologians and "Christian" atheists—the gospel sometimes seems no different from the rhetoric of disbelievers. In a parody of their vocation to offer men the power of the Liberating Word, today's Dionysiac Christians lead men into deeper enshacklement. Rather than calling for the purging fire of God, they dance about the altars of contemporary paganism, scandalizing poor Nietzsche by proclaiming him a Christian prophet!

In the backwash of the "Jesus Revolution," we have been given *Godspell* and *Salvation* and *Jesus Christ Superstar* and "Jesus Is Just All Right with Me" by show business types who neither know nor care why Jesus should be such a hot number. Add to this list Leonard Bernstein's *Mass*, of which the distinguished theatre historian and critic Eric Bentley wrote,

> Bernstein may be said to have known a good thing when he saw it, as could have been said earlier of Cecil B. DeMille when first he looked into the Holy Bible.... This Mass, unlike the one in the church on the corner, is gawked at by persons who have paid, not to worship or otherwise participate, but to gawk.

One is struck also by the terrible disparity between the cynicism of some current singers of popular "Jesus rock" and the dynamic, fervid faith of the late Mahalia Jackson. The jazz critic Nat Hentoff said of her, "The first thing you must realize about singing gospel music is that you can't sing it if you don't believe it. Mahalia Jackson believed every word she sang."

The world sorely needs Christians who believe every word they sing, every word they speak, every word they write because they believe the Word to be true. But it will not be enough merely to announce our faith. We must also redeem the rhetoric of the gospel from the sloppiness and sham of expression in which it too often appears, even in the hands of earnest Christians.

Too few Christians aspiring to proclaim the mystery, to make known the message of the Word, have taken time to study their craft and make certain of the gift. Aristotle laid down a lasting maxim when he wrote, "It is not enough to know *what* we ought to say; we must also say it *as* we ought." Saying it as we ought means being aware of the implied dramatic situation facing every writer. He must realize that through the medium of words-on-paper his voice is speaking to a living audience. How will he address that audience? In what tone of voice will he speak? What authority does he have to address this audience on this subject? The principal question in rhetoric becomes, "How can I best arrange my language to speak effectively to this audience about this subject?"

The Christian writer takes as his model the example of Jesus himself. His rhetoric, as we find it recorded in the four Gospels, exemplifies the best qualities commended in every handbook on style—simplicity, directness, originality, integrity. Jesus is never complex; his language can be understood by his youngest listener. His rhetoric is never fuzzy with circumlocutions; it is always direct. His speech is pictorial without being extravagant, metaphorical without being trite. We have no record that Jesus ever uttered a cliché. He spoke always the honest, right word, with the result that even his antagonists said of him, "No man ever spoke as this man speaks" (John 7:46).

With this example before him, the Christian writer sets out to fulfill his vocation. He must commit himself to the discipline —the hard, physical labor, the backache and wristache and headache—of writing. He must be committed to the efficacy of writing, to its power to transform lives. In short, he must believe in the Word; he must take pride in proclaiming it.

The French novelist and Nobel Prize winner, Francois Mauriac, a devout Christian, has said of himself,

> My writings have benefited from the fact that, no matter how lazy I was, I always wrote the least article with care, putting my whole soul into it. I will have remained all my life the sixth-form student who wants his essay to be better than all the others and to be read aloud in class.

Too few professed Christian writers can say the same of themselves. They are as Jacques Barzun characterized the type: men who "do not want to *write*, they want to *have written!*" Consequently the sense of haste, the absence of style and taste that is the mark of so much writing representative of Christian thought: ecclesiastical jargon, constant overstatement, predictable evangelical cliché, mindless *non sequitur*, fad phrases of an adolescent mentality. Richard Brinsley Sheridan rightly said, "Easy writing makes vile hard reading!"

The Christian writer must do better than this. To begin, the Christian writer needs to see himself from two perspectives. He is, first, a *Christian*, a term which both defines and liberates him. By definition a Christian is someone who has acknowledged the insufficiency of life lived apart from a relationship with God through Jesus Christ. In making that acknowledgment, however, the Christian becomes heir to the whole universe, a participant in the riches to be shared as a child of God with his Son. In this special sense, then, a Christian is a Christian, nothing else. His true vocation is that of a proclaimer of the gospel. He may, as Dwight L. Moody used to say of himself, "mend shoes to meet expenses."

But the Christian who chooses to be a writer is different from the Christian plumber or hardware salesman or lawyer or accountant. Together with them, the Christian writer needs to insure that his personal behavior is exemplary of the believer. He needs to be scrupulous about the standards of his work— avoiding plagiarism, never substituting shoddiness for genuine craftsmanship, fulfilling a commitment to produce one's work when promised. These essential characteristics of the Christian writer are at a level of stewardship which ought to be assumed. Where the Christian writer differs from his counterparts in trades and professions is at a level deeper than these assumptions, differences resulting from the medium in which each works.

For the Christian plumber or the godless plumber alike, the medium is copper piping and the acetylene torch; for the Christian or unchristian hardware salesman, nuts and bolts, paint and varnish; for the Christian or unchristian lawyer, the law and its precedents in judgment; for accountants, whether Christians or unbelievers, standard bookkeeping practice and ledgers. To be sure, occasions arise every day in the experience of the Christian tradesman, the Christian professional, in which he must make a vocational decision that reflects on his faith. But his tools, his wrenches, merchandise, briefs, or balance sheets, are substantively no different from those of the disbeliever.

The Christian writer's tools are words about the Word. In their very choice and shape he is responsible as his fellow Christians in other vocations are not. The words he selects determine not only whether he succeeds as a writer but also whether he succeeds as a Christian. A conscientious yet agnostic plumber may lead a line of pipe as skilfully as a Christian plumber; the householder examining the job cannot tell the difference. The same cannot be said of two equally able writers. In treating the same subject, the point of view of the Christian writer must necessarily cause his work to stand apart from the disbeliever's.

The reason goes beyond word choice. It goes into the roots of rhetoric, the relationship between rhetoric and character. The basis of a man's rhetoric is his total view of life, reduced to the microcosmic dimensions of his present circumstances. This is what is known as the artist's world-view. Because, as Edmund Fuller argues in his book *Man in Modern Fiction*, the subject of art is mankind himself, the primary question to be asked of an artist, a writer, is this: "What is your view of man?"

The late Flannery O'Connor said of herself,

I am no disbeliever in spiritual purpose and no vague believer. I see from the standpoint of Christian orthodoxy. This means that for me the meaning of life is centered in our Redemption by Christ and that what I see in the World I see in its relation to that.

For every Christian writer the view taken of life must be from the vantage of the Cross and the Empty Tomb as the central point of history, as the absolute moment in time. From the foot of the Cross, the Christian writer looks out upon mankind in every state and condition of behavior. He sees the thoughtless and uncaring as they dice away their souls; he sees the blasphemous and contemptuous crying out their scorn; he sees the curious and the uncommitted; he sees believers both living and dying. He hears two great words of grace—"Father, forgive them" and "It is finished."

From the entrance to the Tomb he sees the disinterested and the denying; the fearful and the disbelieving; the intellectual skeptic, the timid doubter. He also sees joy in belief and hears the conquering claim, "The Lord is risen indeed!" From this vision, at the Cross and at the Empty Tomb, the Christian writer obtains his sense of mission.

This view is scarcely a pretty one; it can't be stomached by the Pollyanna or Grace Livingston Hill mentality. It is life stripped of every civilizing mask, life at its most barbaric, life in elemental conflict with death. The Christian's view reveals a God who subjects himself to the supreme indignity—the Creator fettered by the creature. As in Poe's nightmare poem "The Conqueror Worm," the spectacle of the Cross contains "much of Madness, and more of Sin, / And Horror the soul of the plot." At Calvary, the worm turns.

But this is only a partial view and not the complete Christian vision because it omits the qualifying factor, namely, the willingness of Jesus Christ to accept the ignominy of the Cross. What the Christian sees, therefore, is more than a noble but tragic martyr, more than a Frog-Prince willing to die so that Swans may become princesses; more than a dying god whose sacrifice is a mythic necessity. What the Christian sees and thereafter feels compelled to proclaim is that the titanic combat between the forces of Satan and the Trinity has been resolved forever.

The territory of the Cross is a war zone. As such it presents a terrifying prospect to anyone who doesn't understand that the final victory has been won, that the Seed of the Woman has finally trampled down the head of the Serpent. But until his writhing ends, the Serpent continues to deceive many into believing him to be the victor.

The greatest evidence contradicting the Serpent comes not at the Cross but from the Empty Tomb, from the fact of the Resurrection. If the Cross means tragedy, the Empty Tomb means triumph. If the Cross is shrouded in preternatural darkness, the Empty Tomb radiates with light—the quickening Light of Life.

This is the Christian's message, but to tell it plainly he must describe his vision in all its reality, balancing light with darkness. For him there can be no Sunday School stories of meadowlands and flowers, of good deeds by loving children and philanthropic acts by kind adults, without also reckoning with the presence of sin in human experience. The greatest writers know this to be so. Herman Melville, explaining the genius of his friend Nathaniel Hawthorne, attributed Hawthorne's power to his recognition of the doctrines of Innate Depravity and Original Sin, "from whose visitations," said Melville, "in some shape or other, no deeply thinking mind is always and wholly free."

Flannery O'Connor has rightly observed that "writers who see by the light of their Christian faith will have, in these times, the sharpest eyes for the grotesque, for the perverse, for the unacceptable." This is so because the Christian writer can't deny the lingering aftermath of the Fall, the fact that the Scriptures teach that mankind is alienated from God and at odds with his purposes. The Christian writer can't write as though the Cross had never been needed or raised, because the Christian writer is responsible to urge men to kneel before the crucified Son of God. He can't write as though the Tomb were still sealed, because he is committed to bring men face to face with the Risen Lord.

This won't be done unless men are made dramatically aware of their position with regard to God and Satan, their need to make a lasting choice between life and death. "Knowing therefore the terror of the Lord, we persuade men," said St. Paul (2 Corinthians 5:11, KJV). In other words, a rhetoric of straightforward and unmistakable clarity, a rhetoric that tells the whole truth about God and men, time and eternity, good and evil—a rhetoric empowered by the very strength of God.

St. Augustine, in his treatise *On Christian Doctrine*, gave instruction for such a rhetoric:

> It is the duty, then, of the interpreter and teacher of Holy Scripture, the defender of the true faith and the opponent of error, both to teach what is right and to refute what is wrong, and in the performance of this task to conciliate the hostile, to rouse the careless, and to tell the ignorant both what is occurring at present and what is probable in the future. . . . If, however, the hearers require to be

roused rather than instructed, in order that they may be diligent to do what they already know, and to bring their feelings into harmony with the truths they admit, greater vigor of speech is needed. Here entreaties and reproaches, exhortations and upbraidings, and all the other means of rousing the emotions are necessary.

In this same spirit of urgency, Flannery O'Connor called for the Christian writer to make modern life's repugnant features "appear as distortions to an audience which is used to seeing them as natural." She went on,

When you can assume that your audience holds the same beliefs you do, you can relax a little and use more normal ways of talking to it; when you have to assume that it does not, then you have to make your vision apparent by shock—to the hard of hearing you shout, and for the almost blind you draw large and startling figures.

To make one's vision apparent by shock may require shocking tactics—the use of language and incident unbecoming to the Christian but routinely part of the behavior of men and women at odds with God. The Christian writer is committed to telling the truth. He doesn't meet that obligation by avoiding life's realities or by circumventing them. The novelist who brings a drunken villain to an attractive woman's door and lets his character's intentions be known by his beating on a barred door, shows his own lack of nerve when he gives the attempted rapist nothing stronger to say than "Gadfry" and "You slut."

Clyde S. Kilby comments on the necessity of realism in art when he writes,

There is no comprehending of light until we have somehow suffered the intensity of darkness, no comprehending of freedom apart from the circumscription of slavery.... Can the Christian ever be a true witness to his neighbor until he comprehends the sin which captivates his neighbor, until with some vividness he imagines his neighbor different from what he is now? ... In fact, apart from such imaginative participation, will not one's neighbor become mere spiritual merchandise, mere object-to-be-saved, to whom a formula of regeneration is indiscriminately spoken robot-fashion and apart from genuine sympathy and love?

The fine line between necessary realism and unnecessary obsession with filth and crime must be decided individually by each writer, each reader. But the pious who shake their heads at the Christian writer's portrayal of evil should remember that the omniscient God incarnate in Jesus Christ did not enter upon the act of redemption until after he had come to witness at first hand the sins of drunkards, thieves, prostitutes, and madmen.

This doesn't mean that the Christian writer may, on the other hand, tilt the balance toward sexual voyeurism or a psychopathic fixation upon violence. He must be certain that his audience can recognize in him the difference between truth and titillation. Freedom to tell the whole truth about the wretchedness of sin must not exceed the same writer's capacity to express the grandeur of redemption. Such an axiom places a strong curb on the writer's license to indulge his yearning for realism because it will always be easier to portray men's baseness than their striving for God. Somehow profanity in speech always seems more "real" than expressions of praise to God; descriptions of illicit sexual relations stimulate one's imagination more readily than do descriptions of participation in Holy Communion.

In his book *The Christian Mind*, Harry Blamires reminds us of the paradox that "flowers grow best in manured soil." The Christian artist understands the tension between beauty and filth; he knows the reality of each. Because of his biblical view of man's condition, he can't deny the foulness of the Garden, now "rank and gross in nature," as Hamlet says. But when it comes time for the Christian writer to rearrange and compose nature through his art, he reaches for the flowers, not the fertilizer.

The Christian writer must struggle hard to find a proper distribution of the elements of "realism," keeping in mind that his purpose isn't to glamorize "realism," but to glorify God.

* * *

The work of O'Connor provides a useful example of a writer's attempt to make her vision apparent by shock. The manner in which she goes about fulfilling her purpose deliberately overturns most readers' preconceptions of what to expect from a young, unmarried, devoutly believing Roman Catholic woman writing in the American South during the 1950s and into the 1960s. Under the typical categories, one might assume that such a writer would concentrate upon aspects of life narrowly constricted by her own experience. But among the truest indicators of genuine literature is its universality. Although O'Connor's novels and almost all her stories are set in the rural South she knew so well, in every other respect she upsets our categories.

She does not write specifically about the young, except to reveal in them the cruelty of youth toward age. In fact, few of her best drawn characters are young people; rather, we meet a succession of respectable matrons—Mrs. Chestny, Mrs. Hope-well, Mrs. May, Mrs. Fox, Mrs. Turpin—and a few downtrodden men—Mr. Shiftlet, O. E. Parker, W. T. Tanner. When dealing with the relationships between generations, it's not the domestic struggle between mother and spinster daughter with which she copes; more often, such family problems are between mother and son—Mrs. Chestny and Julian in "Everything That Rises Must Converge," Mrs. Fox and Asbury in "The Enduring Chill," his mother and Thomas in "The Comforts of Home."

In order to show a world that has come to accept disorder in place of order, O'Connor tells of the greater chaos she sees. She exposes the horrors of lovelessness and spite, beating plati-tudes about family life upon the anvil of reality. Grown sons express openly their contempt for the genteel ways of their earnest, hard-working (often widowed) mothers, deliberately venting upon them the frustrations of their own impotence and unfulfillment. The women whine in return. "I work and slave, I struggle and sweat to keep this place for them and soon as I'm dead, they'll marry trash and bring it here and ruin every-thing I've done," says Mrs. May of her two grown no-account sons in "Greenleaf."

For Mrs. May the impending disaster she faces is the collapse of social castes and of the inviolable laws of association—white above black, "decent folks" above "trash." This latter category preoccupies the minds of several of O'Connor's desperate women, more than any unthinkable prospect of an interracial marriage, which one mother considers "the ultimate horror." Mrs. Chestny comforts herself that in spite of social upheaval, "If you know who you are, you can go anywhere":

> "Your great-grandfather was a former governor of this state," she said [to her son Julian]. "Your grandfather was a prosperous land-owner. Your grandmother was a Godhigh."
>
> "Will you look around you," he said tensely, "and see where you are now?" and he swept his arm jerkily out to indicate the neigh-borhood, which the growing darkness at least made less dingy.
>
> "You remain what you are," she said. "Your great-grandfather had a plantation and two hundred slaves."

In another story, "Revelation," the self-righteous Mrs. Turpin passes through a wrenching moment in a doctor's office. She has been sitting quietly observing the other waiting patients, smugly locating each on a social ladder, continuing a personal game.

> Sometimes at night when she couldn't go to sleep, Mrs. Turpin would occupy herself with the question of who she would have chosen to be if she couldn't have been herself. If Jesus had said to her before he made her, "There's only two places available for you. You either be a nigger or white-trash," what would she have said?

Always Mrs. Turpin's decision, in such moments of anxiety, is the same: " 'All right, make me a nigger then—but that don't mean a trashy one.' And he would have made her a neat clean respectable Negro woman, herself but black." Of course, Mrs. Turpin is only fantasizing. The glorious fact, for her, is that Jesus "had not made her a nigger or white-trash or ugly! He had made her herself and given her a little of everything. Jesus, thank you!"

But while Mrs. Turpin so muses on her favored status with God and with society, an ugly, acne-covered girl from Wellesley College attacks her, assaulting her in the doctor's waiting room. The physical humiliation is bad enough, but the girl (O'Connor names her Mary Grace) also abuses Mrs. Turpin by telling her, "Go back to hell where you came from, you old wart hog."

Mrs. Turpin's husband Claud takes her home, where in the late afternoon she stands by the rail of her immaculate pigpen. There she has a momentary vision. She sees the whole range of her social order—white trash, blacks, freaks and lunatics, as well as people like herself—marching toward Heaven. The procession is disorganized and random, except for her kind of people. O'Connor writes:

> They alone were on key. Yet she could see by their shocked and altered faces that even their virtues were being burned away. She lowered her hands and gripped the rail of the hog pen, her eyes small but fixed unblinkingly on what lay ahead. In a moment the vision faded but she remained where she was, immobile.

What Mrs. Turpin has seen is a visionary foretaste of the equality in Heaven. There no social ladder exists, no register records the status and caste of the heavenly. "Who is the greatest in the kingdom of heaven?" Certainly not the self-righteous, the bigoted, the man or woman who sets great store by social position in life. Flannery O'Connor leaves no doubt of this truth.

Yet throughout "Revelation," as throughout most of her

works, she has seemed to be saying exactly the opposite—and this is another means by which O'Connor reverses her reader's expectations. To make her vision apparent by shock she practices the craft of paradox with needle-point precision. Paradox, said G. K. Chesterton, is "Truth standing on its head to get attention." Explicit truth is often too commonplace; preachy truth dilutes into a didactic moral lesson. "Tell all the Truth but tell it slant," Emily Dickinson advised, and Flannery O'Connor follows that advice.

In doing so she also follows the example of One who taught by paradox and parable. D. Elton Trueblood says, "Christ's use of paradox is dazzling. The entire process of finding similarity in apparent difference, which makes parable possible, is deeply paradoxical." The paradoxes which Jesus spoke began in aphorism and extended to human experience. Many of his teachings can be summed up in the concept of finding versus losing as perhaps the essential paradox of the Christian experience. Two examples come readily to mind: Jesus said, "Whoever cares for his own safety is lost; but if a man will let himself be lost for my sake, he will find his true self" (Matthew 16:25), a famous statement of paradox whereby all the values of materialism are discredited and spiritual integrity is rewarded.

The other example is the famous parable of the Prodigal Son, perhaps more accurately called the parable of the Two Brothers. The younger brother, the so-called Prodigal, loses everything—inheritance, friends, respectability, almost his life. But by an act of contrition he finds, first, the unfailing love of his father and also the restoration of the best of all he had lost. For him, through sad and bitter experience, losing was the only way ultimately to find. His brother, on the contrary, discovers too late—if at all—that what he had never valued is now precious to him. He has lost the fatted calf; he now finds that he would have been happy to have shared a bit of goat-meat with his friends.

By life and by death Jesus Christ exemplified the existential reality of the paradox of finding and losing. This, after all, is the definitive meaning of the Cross and the Empty Tomb, that death brings life. It is the insistent irony of our faith.

Flannery O'Connor allows the rhetoric of paradox and irony to have full play in her stories, turning many of them into outright counter-parables. Consider "The Life You Save May Be

Your Own" as a counter-parable of the Good Samaritan. Here an opportunist named Tom T. Shiftlet bilks a crafty old redneck woman out of her automobile by promising to marry the woman's idiot daughter. Shiftlet fulfills his promise, but having then conned the mother into paying for a honeymoon ("I wouldn't marry the Duchesser Windsor unless I could take her to a hotel and give her something good to eat"), he abandons the girl in a roadside diner. As he proceeds on his way toward Mobile, he passes the billboard caution of the National Safety Council, "The life you save may be your own." This is the motto of Shiftlet's despicable career, the living antithesis of Christ's commandment about losing-in-order-to-find. No wonder that as Shiftlet drives into Mobile "a guffawing peal of thunder" echoes in his ears, like the derisive laughter of Almighty God.

It would be hard to imagine a more Christian story than this; yet Flannery O'Connor has achieved her purpose, to convey the truth about the world's distortions, without so much as a Christian cliché getting in the way of her message. She has pushed her reader to the edge of absurdity but drawn him back in time for the weight of the culminating biblical allusion to a laughing God to crush any thoughtless hilarity. This use of the absurd, the preposterous, one finds throughout her work: in "Good Country People," the scheming Bible salesman who seduces the girl with both a Ph. D. and a wooden leg, then places the leg out of the cripple's easy reach; or the brutality of the paranoid killer, named The Misfit, in "A Good Man Is Hard to Find." Here a garrulous mother-in-law talks her son-in-law into taking a back country road to see an old homestead—which she later remembers is actually in another state! On the deserted road the family is set upon by The Misfit and his gang. The desperadoes eventually execute them, one by one. When it is the old woman's turn,

> She saw the man's face twisted close to her own as if he were going to cry and she murmured, "Why you're one of my babies. You're one of my own children!" She reached out and touched him on the shoulder. The Misfit sprang back as if a snake had bitten him and shot her three times through the chest. Then he put his gun down on the ground and took off his glasses and began to clean them.

Surely O'Connor's greatest accomplishment in developing a rhetoric of the gospel through paradox, irony, and absurdity is in her novel *Wise Blood*. This bizarre work may seem at first

too grotesque to be credible. It centers upon the efforts of Hazel
(or Haze) Motes, a self-appointed evangelist. In a parody of
institutionalized religion, Haze Motes searches for a new Jesus
to lead his "Church of Christ Without Christ." He finds only
a shrunken mummy from a museum showcase.

On its surface *Wise Blood* is a comic success, although
O'Connor's art always rises above ridicule; indeed, it often
approaches the level of Greek tragedy in its power to evoke from
the audience both pity and fear. In this case in particular the
correspondence with tragic drama is unmistakable because *Wise
Blood* so closely parallels Sophocles' play *Oedipus the King*. In
the play the controlling metaphors for opposite degrees of self-
understanding and salvation are *sight* and *blindness, darkness*
and *light*. Haze Motes (his name suggests a bleared vision) is
told by a blind prophet, in a speech echoing Tiresias' condemnation of Oedipus, "I can see more than you! You got eyes and
see not, ears and hear not, but you'll have to see some time."
By the novel's end, Motes like Oedipus has blinded himself.

Many of O'Connor's characters are starkly real products of
the Bible-belt, quivering with an emotionalism known as religious fervor, quaking with an opposite dread of having missed
salvation. But her saints and sinners are no stereotypes. They
exceed anything one may see on early Sunday morning television
in Southern cities or hear screeching through the night from
"country" radio stations.

Strangely, Flannery O'Connor wrote little about Roman
Catholics, although she was herself a faithful daughter of the
Church. The only prominent place given to a Roman Catholic
priest occurs in "The Enduring Chill," a story about a foolish
and frustrated aspiring writer whose hypochondria has brought
him home to Georgia from New York City, presumably to die.
His name is Asbury Fox, an obviously Protestant name. He
demands to see a Jesuit priest because in New York he had met
a priest who had "appealed to him as a man of the world,
someone who would have understood the unique tragedy of his
death." Reluctantly his Methodist mother yields to the intrusion
of a priest into her home.

And what kind of entry does O'Connor allow this representative of Mother Church? Father Finn is blind in one eye, almost
totally deaf, has never heard of James Joyce, and can only
parrot the Church's hackneyed responses in catechizing Asbury's

soul. By this decision O'Connor, far from downgrading the Church in which she worshipped almost daily and through whose mediation she knew Jesus Christ as her Lord, seems to be saying that a religious experience must be authentic; it cannot be the result of a purely emotional encounter. Just as Asbury's supposed fatal illness is sham—he has contracted undulant fever from drinking unpasteurized milk in his mother's barn, then offered it to her black workmen—so too has been his attraction to Romanism. Both are the result of his affected liberalism, an adolescent attempt at severing the silver cord by cultural shock. O'Connor is showing that the only route to true salvation is that of honest self-abnegation before God, often at the risk of personal catastrophe.

Flannery O'Connor herself wrote out of the fires of faith triumphant over physical anguish and disability. She wrote the major portion of her work while suffering from a painful and disfiguring disease, disseminated lupus, that in time took her life, at age thirty-nine. But suffering did not deaden her gift; if anything, her pain seemed to equip her with an acuteness of perception that made it possible for her to compress into the story form what other writers needed the novel's length to say. "She touched the bone of truth that was sunk in her own flesh," says Alfred Kazin. O'Connor knew in the same physical terms what Job meant when he cried out in his torment, "After my skin has been thus destroyed, then from my flesh I shall see God" (Job 19:26 RSV). She knew—and she wrote out of the surety of this knowledge—that seeing God was the ultimate vision to be had by any human being. By the power of her gift for rhetoric, she enabled her readers to see the futility of life apart from God's enveloping love.

Teilhard de Chardin, from whom O'Connor took the title of her story "Everything That Rises Must Converge," corroborated O'Connor's recognition of the necessity of God's love. In a statement that anticipates and goes beyond Charles Reich's several levels of "Consciousness," Teilhard writes of "a specifically new state of consciousness." He was thinking of Christian love.

> Christian love is incomprehensible to those who have not experienced it. That the infinite and the intangible can be lovable, or that the human heart can beat with genuine charity for a fellow-being, seems impossible to many people I know—in fact almost monstrous. But

whether it be founded on an illusion or not, how can we doubt that
such a sentiment exists, and even in great intensity? We have only
to note crudely the results it produces unceasingly around us.

Because the nature of her rhetoric depends so greatly upon
irony, paradox, and the absurd, some of O'Connor's readers
have not found it easy to identify in her stories the Christian
love and compassion to which she points. Careful readers have
found the quality of her faith, however, as may be observed in
the fact that her work has twice received posthumously the
National Book Award, in 1966 and again in 1972, eight years
after her death.

On the first occasion the judges wrote that Flannery O'Connor's work "commands our memory with sensations of life
conveyed with an intensity of pity and participation, love and
redemption, rarely encountered." At the publishing of her
Complete Stories, Alfred Kazin wrote, "Reading her, one is
aware above all of a gift blessedly made objective." This gift
Flannery O'Connor gave back to God and to us all in a rhetoric
matching the character of her life.

CHAPTER SIX

the pen of a ready writer

More than a few readers have been guilty of overreading a passage in literature to the point that the basic sense of the work crumbles into a symbolic hash. Works with religious themes are especially susceptible to complicated misreadings and labyrinthine explications. Almost always such analyses depend upon suffocating plot summaries and the most rococo examples of associative reasoning.

I have no wish to enlarge any further the abundance of such books about Christian writers. But I feel an obligation, having come this far with my analysis, to discuss three additional writers whose art is offered in service to the glory of God. I can best do this, I think, by confining my examples, limiting my scope to treat only well-known works.

* * *

I begin with Graham Greene, an English novelist and playwright who at age twenty-two was converted to Roman Catholicism. Like Flannery O'Connor in America, however, Greene has deliberately avoided allowing his art to become tractarian. He is no propagandist for the Roman Church; indeed, to many Christians, his doctrine may be heterodoxy, if not outright heresy. He is an apologist for "the appalling strangeness of the mercy of God," mediated through the sacraments of the Church and the lives of common men.

The mercy of God may be taken as one of Greene's convictions about the nature of God's dealings with men. To give substance to God's mercy, or at least to the human view of its necessity, Greene often places before his reader characters of little moral worth—except, of course, to God. Again like O'Connor, he populates his fiction with grotesques: a teenaged

hoodlum in *Brighton Rock* who makes the petty bullies of
Anthony Burgess' *A Clockwork Orange* appear like choirboys;
a whisky priest in *The Power and the Glory* consuming the
Body and Blood in a state of mortal sin; a despairing architect
in *A Burnt-Out Case* who retreats to the isolation of a lepro-
sarium; an honest policeman in *The Heart of the Matter* whose
adultery drives him to suicide, "the worst crime a Catholic
could commit"; a doctor in *The Honorary Consul* who sees himself, like Pilate, delivering into the hands of guerrillas the life
of an innocent man.

Each of these apparently hopeless and helpless persons is
also, however, to be seen fulfilling his place in the Kingdom of
God, for Greene will have no truck with anarchy or the belief
in a God so weak as to be fettered by human willfulness. "Thine
is the kingdom," we are taught to pray; if this is so, then the
power and the glory follow in their natural order. Implicit, therefore, in Greene's fiction (as one may infer from the title of his
best known novel, *The Power and the Glory*) is the belief that
"the kingdoms of this world are become the kingdoms of our
Lord, and of His Christ" (Revelation 11:15, KJV).

Thus all these Roman Catholics come to know, through
some means or other, the mercy of God, although as Sarah
says in *The End of the Affair*, "It's such an odd sort of mercy,
it sometimes looks like punishment." For Sarah, a collapsed love
affair brings her to realize the near presence of God. "You were
there," she tells God in her diary, "teaching us to squander . . .
so that one day we might have nothing left except this love of
You." For the dissolute priest, facing death by a dictator's firing
squad, the prospect brings him a sense of "immense disappoint-
ment because he had to go to God empty-handed, with nothing
done at all." Querry the architect is murdered by a jealous but
mistaken husband, but before his death he has ceased to be "a
burnt-out case," cured by the touch of love. These are some of
the acts of mercy meted out by God's grace.

As is true of any genuine artist, Greene has the power of
taking a reader into the very center of a character's soul, there
making the reader participate in the struggle being fought. In
the case of Pinkie, the adolescent terrorizer of *Brighton Rock*,
the conflict Greene establishes focuses upon an absurd paradox:
Pinkie must decide between the concepts of Good-and-Evil
taught him by priests in the moral sterility of a classroom, or

the reality of Right-and-Wrong learned in the school playground, the city's streets, the lairs of criminals.

Pinkie resolves the paradox in favor of Evil, his Good, because he decides "he wasn't made for peace, he couldn't believe in it." To Pinkie, "Heaven was a word; Hell was something he could trust. A brain was capable only of what it could conceive, and it couldn't conceive what it had never experienced." All he had ever known was Hell. "Why, this is Hell," Marlowe's Mephistopheles had told Doctor Faustus, "nor are we out of it." Yet Life-as-Hell is not enough Hell for Pinkie's delight. "It's jail," he cries, "and not knowing where to get some money. Worms and cataract, cancer. You hear 'em shrieking from the upper windows—children being born. It's dying slowly." Pinkie prefers Death and a Hell far more liquid and unremitting than any the priests had warned against.

He chooses Death and Hell over capture by the police, jumping over a Channel cliff "as if he'd been withdrawn suddenly by a hand out of any existence—past or present, whipped away into zero—nothing."

But Graham Greene withholds from Pinkie his absolute certainty of damnation, detecting the mercy of God even in all this mayhem. A priest tells Pinkie's wife, "The Church does not demand that we believe any soul is cut off from mercy." Still troubled, she replies, "He's damned. He knew what he was about. He was a Catholic too." But still the priest holds out hope, explaining an important Christian tenet:

> I mean—a Catholic is more capable of evil than anyone. I think perhaps—because we believe in him—we are more in touch with the devil than other people. But we must hope, hope and pray. . . . If he loved you, surely, that shows there was some good.

What Greene is saying through the priest is that while it is true for the Christian that God is goodness and love and rules supreme in the universe, this thesis has also its antithesis. Evil is a present force, and no one knows this better than the man who loves God. A naturalist denying the existence or the efficacy of God in the face of evil would claim a synthesis of even greater evil. But a Christian novelist—a Francois Mauriac, a Graham Greene—sees the inexplicable power of God as sufficient cause for hope.

This same indomitable faith in the mercy of God shines through the best of Greene's novels, *The Heart of the Matter*.

The essence of the Christian message is that "it is not the healthy that need a doctor, but the sick." Jesus didn't come to invite virtuous people into the Kingdom of God, "but to call sinners to repentance" (Luke 5:32). This truth shows first in Greene's choice of an epigraph for his novel, a statement from the writings of Charles Peguy, a French Socialist and poet at the beginning of this century, whose conversion to Christian belief made him a spokesman for the faith: "The sinner is at heart the same as Christendom. . . . No one is as competent as the sinner in the matter of Christendom. No one, if it's not the saint."

A hidden irony pervades the choice of this quotation, for Peguy, like the protagonist of this novel, had experienced the anguish of love for a young woman not his wife. Like Greene's policeman Henry Scobie, Peguy felt driven to the borders of spiritual despair. Unlike Scobie, however, Peguy found peace in the Scriptural promise, "My grace is all you need; power comes to its full strength in weakness" (2 Corinthians 12:9).

Police Inspector Henry Scobie—"Scobie the Just"—is Greene's paradigm for modern man. Essentially a person of responsibility and courage, he yields to deceit and cowardice only because his pity replaces his principles. It's a progression downward possible only in a good man—the faithful Catholic who reverences the Mass, the Wine and the Wafer. "Only the man of good will," writes Greene, "carries always in his heart this capacity for damnation." Only the man to whom the Blood of Christ means something can know the terror of rejecting its atoning power. "O God," Scobie mourns, "I've killed you."

What begins in pity for a helpless widow soon turns to a relationship "condemned to consequences" because of Scobie's inescapable sense of responsibility. Now he discovers that he's possessed by two contradictory responsibilities—to his wife Louise and to Helen, the woman he loves. In addition, he has his love of God. Yet, he asks, "how can one love God at the expense of one of his creatures?"

Once convicted by his mortal sin of adultery, Scobie at first refuses to compound his guilt by taking communion while in an unrepentant state. "It's striking God when he's down," he explains to Helen. As a Catholic he knows the answers to all the questions raised by his struggling conscience. But he can't stop seeing Helen, and he can't refuse to accompany Louise to church without offering her a reasonable excuse. And so he commits himself to the easier alternative—to damnation, "with the pale papery taste of his eternal sentence on the tongue."

But Scobie can't continue. "I want to stop giving pain," he tells Helen. To God he says, "I love you and I won't go on insulting you at your own altar." Already damned, he decides to commit the unforgivable sin, suicide. "I'm a responsible man," he says to himself, "and I'll see it through the only way I can."

Greene offers no romantic illusions about Scobie's suicide. It isn't the end, as he and every thinking man with Hamlet knows. Nor is it part of the myth of eternal return, the desire to start all over again, a new beginning. It is "an eternity of deprivation." "This was what human love had done to him— it had robbed him of love for eternity. It was no use pretending as a young man might that the price was worthwhile."

Here, then, is Scobie's despair. Yet just before he takes the overdose of pills, he hears the voice of God pleading with him.

> You say you love me, and yet you do this to me—rob me of you for ever. I made you with love. I've wept your tears. I've saved you from more than you will ever know; I planted in you this longing for peace only so that one day I could satisfy your longing and watch your happiness. And now you push me away, you put me out of your reach.

He dies, ironically, unnecessarily, for after his death Greene lets us know that Louise has known about Scobie's affair for some time. She goes in her self-righteous affrontedness to Father Rank, hoping for priestly consolation. "It's no good even praying," she says. His reply shocks her.

> "For goodness' sake, Mrs. Scobie, don't imagine you—or I— know a thing about God's mercy."
> "The Church says . . ."
> "I know the Church says. The Church knows all the rules. But it doesn't know what goes on in a single human heart."

Father Rank is convinced about Scobie that "he really loved God." As readers made privy to Scobie's dialogues, we can agree, while at the same time recognizing that Scobie's moral *cul-de-sac* is of his own making. He could have loved God more by loving Helen Rolt less! Yet Graham Greene has demonstrated once more that the mystery of grace remains beyond our comprehension, as well as beyond our legislation. It remains "the appalling strangeness of the mercy of God," mercy that characterizes God's dealings with men since Adam. For Genesis shows—and Greene illustrates in his fiction—that in spite of Man's disobedience, God continues to provide for the human race's well-being and eventual restoration. The animal skins that clothed Adam and Eve, the distinguishing mark on Cain, the ark of safety, and the rainbow covenant were all demonstrations of God's unending mercy for generations yet to come.

In Greene's work too, the extension of God's mercy is passed along to succeeding generations. *Brighton Rock* closes with Pinkie's widow, carrying their unborn child, being advised by the priest to raise the child to pray for his father. The effect on the young widow reveals Greene's spiritual hope: "A sudden feeling of immense gratitude broke through the pain—it was as if she had been given the sight a long way off of life going on again." Again, in spite of the whisky priest's despair that his life has been worthless, he has all unknowingly confirmed the faith of a fourteen-year-old boy, so that as *The Power and the Glory* ends the boy is helping another priest to survive.

Even in *A Burnt-Out Case*, where Greene seems to be most ambiguous about a personal theology of grace, he makes the medical metaphor stand for spiritual life or death. One of the missionary priests says, "Belief without grace is unthinkable, and God will never rob a man of grace. Only a man himself can do that—by his own actions." By his actions, through his "heroic virtue," the disbelieving architect Querry has contributed to the building of a leprosy hospital, so that a three-year-old child infected with the physical disease can be treated and promised a cure without permanent mutilation. Greene would have his reader understand that "God's arm is not so short that he cannot save, nor his ear too dull to hear" (Isaiah 59:1). It's a comforting doctrine, especially to any who have known at first hand God's mercy, to know that it extends equally to others. This too is part of the Christian writer's vision, obtained by his view of the world from the foot of the Cross, and from the vacated Tomb.

Greene's 1973 bestselling novel, *The Honorary Consul*, consolidates many of his previous themes in a masterly way. Here again we find the need of every man for love and security, the struggle between cold intellectuality and human passion, and questions over the perplexing nature of God. As usual, Greene's central character is a man alienated, both politically and emotionally, from the society in which he lives. Eduardo Plarr, the

son of an English father and Latin-American mother, yearns
for a relationship stripped from him at fourteen years by his
father's revolutionary acts against the Paraguayan dictatorship.
Now thirty-four years old, Doctor Plarr still has not reconciled
himself to being fatherless. He stands by the river's edge, on
the Argentine side, looking across to the shore where he had
last seen his father—an exile, disoriented and lost.

Plarr is also an emotional cripple, incapable of love, whether
for his mother—a faded Spanish beauty whose pouchy cheeks
are bloated with whipped-cream eclairs—or any of his several
mistresses. He has never found it possible to say, "I love you";
indeed, he considers the phrase theatrical. Green describes
Plarr's frigidity:

> He had been accused often enough of cruelty, though he preferred to
> think of himself as a painstaking and accurate diagnostician. If for
> once he had been aware of a sickness he could describe in no other
> terms, he would have unhesitatingly used the phrase, "I love," but
> he had always been able to attribute the emotion he felt to a quite
> different malady — to loneliness, pride, physical desire, or even a
> simple sense of curiosity.

Easy seduction is no compensation, however, for the gnawing
at his soul. As a lapsed Roman Catholic, Plarr has rejected
the Church, but much to his dismay he discovers that he still
needs the companionship of other men. In particular, he associ-
ates out of habit, out of necessity, with three men. Jorge Julio
Saavedra, a novelist and sometime patient, is Plarr's sole contact with the world of letters and culture in this unnamed
Argentine city. Saavedra's novels are melodramatic treatises
upon *machismo*, the honored Latin virtue of manly courage and
bravado. Plarr finds their sameness depressing and their code
of living unreal. He longs to correct his patient's distorted vision
of life by telling him, "Life isn't like that. Life isn't noble or
dignified. Even Latin-American life. Nothing is ineluctable. Life
has surprises. Life is absurd. Because it's absurd there is always
hope. Why, one day we may even discover a cure for cancer
and the common cold."

No such remedy is found, but by this novel's end Eduardo
Plarr has traced to inescapable conclusions the surprises and
absurdities that linger in hope.

Plarr's other occasional companions are the only remaining
Englishmen in the region, a decrepit dilettante named Hum-

phries and sixty-one-year-old Charley Fortnum, the Honorary Consul. Humphries provides Plarr with little in the way of intellectual stimulation and Charley Fortnum even less. An expatriate planter, Fortnum has slipped into the wholly meaningless role of Honorary Consul for the British Foreign Office; from this shadow-office he obtains some few perquisites in spite of the fact that he has been known to hoist the Union Jack upside down. An occasional dignitary comes to the north, and the Honorary Consul has the privilege of entertaining him on behalf of the Queen.

But Charley Fortnum's highest satisfaction comes from his young wife Clara, a whore whom he has taken from Señora Sanchez's business establishment and promoted to mistress of the plantation and wife of the Honorary Consul, much to the consternation of the British Ambassador in Buenos Aires. Moreover, at his advanced age Fortnum is also delighted to know that Clara is with child. It never occurs to him that the father of the child might be Clara's attending physician, Doctor Eduardo Plarr.

Such complications in a Greene novel are typical, but here an added filigree: A band of Paraguayan revolutionaries bungles the kidnapping of the American Ambassador and captures instead the worthless Honorary Consul. The leader of the kidnappers is a former Jesuit priest now defrocked but unable to demit his priesthood. As Providence would seem to dictate, Father Rivas is Eduardo Plarr's former schoolboy friend Leon; and among Leon's list of political demands, or so he claims, is the liberation of Plarr's father.

The vice of conflicting pressures tightens upon Plarr as the novel screws to the wincing point. At once, he is amused at the mischance that threatens Fortnum's life and sees in its inevitable collapse—for the British Foreign Office has no intention of capitulating to bandits merely to save a posturing and embarrassing Honorary Consul—the probability of a continued liaison with Clara. At the same time, he hopes for his father's release from languishing in some Paraguayan prison, which release, of course, would bring about Charley Fortnum's safe deliverance.

In the skilled hands of Graham Greene, such a plot spins from muddy formlessness into a vessel of shapely beauty. It becomes the story of fatherhood and paternal love groping for expression, even in the grossest of human relationships—the

missing elder Plarr and his son Eduardo; Plarr and his unborn
bastard child; cuckolded Charley Fortnum and his supposed off-
spring in Clara's womb; eventually and paradoxically, even
Fortnum and Plarr together in an oxymoronic state of hatred
and love, like father and son; Father Rivas and his spiritual sons
of thunder and revolt. And at the highest scale—as well as at
its most blasphemous—Greene shows us the horror of God the
Father and his sons, a Manichean deity as evil as he is good,
as dark as he is light, as hateful as he is loving—in other words,
a Father like all the fathers sons have ever known. This is
Greene's portrait of God reduced by human reasoning to human
frailty.

Trapped in a stinking hut along with the political hostage,
Plarr hears his half-crazed captor, Father Rivas, expound his
revolutionary theology:

> I believe in the evil of God, but I believe in His goodness too. . . .
> He made us in His image — and so our evil is His evil too. How
> could I love God if He were not like me? . . . The God I believe in
> must be responsible for all the evil as well as for all the saints. He
> has to be a God made in our image with a night side as well as a
> day side. . . .
> But I believe in Christ, I believe in the Cross and the Redemption.
> The Redemption of God as well as of Man. . . . We belong to Him
> and He belongs to us.

As Leon sees it, the Father is helpless until rescued and redeemed by the Son.

This is the novelist Saavedra's *machismo* raised to cosmic
proportions—the derring-do that motivates Man to defend God
against dishonoring himself, that launches a commando assault
against Evil, that willingly sacrifices oneself as a Son in order
to save the Father.

When at last Leon admits that to purchase Plarr's collabora-
tion he has lied about Plarr's father (killed a year before while
trying to escape prison), Plarr transfers his filial loyalty from
his own father to Charley Fortnum. Like the Son yielding up
his life while the Father turns his back upon him, Eduardo Plarr
steps from the barricaded hovel in an effort to save the Honorary Consul's life. He is shot fatally by the uncompromising
troops, but as he lies wounded he hears the voice of Leon, who
has followed him and also been shot:

> A whisper came from behind him.
> Doctor Plarr said, "I can't hear you."

The voice said a word which sounded like "Father." Nothing in their situation seemed to make any sense whatever.

"Lie still," Doctor Plarr said. "If they see either of us move they may shoot again. Don't even speak."

"I am sorry . . . I beg pardon . . ."

"Ego te absolvo," Doctor Plarr whispered in a flash of memory. He intended to laugh, to show Leon he was only joking — they had often joked when they were boys at the unmeaning formulas the priests taught them to see — but he was too tired and the laugh shriveled in his throat.

The exchange of roles—petitioner for priest, son for father—is complete but for one addition. In the novel's epilogue, when Charley Fortnum asks Clara to suggest a name for the child he now knows to be Plarr's, she dutifully urges "Charley." But her husband replies, "One Charley's enough in the family. I think we will call him Eduardo. You see I loved Eduardo in a way. He was young enough to be my son."

Yet for all his genius as a novelist, one wonders whether Greene has been overmastered here by mere sentimentality. Have Eduardo and Leon been, in fact, redeemed without re-affirming their abandoned faith? Or was the gesture of each—Plarr's on behalf of Fortnum, Father Rivas' on behalf of Plarr—sufficient to merit grace? By Greene's theology, faith is manifest only through works. Thus *The Honorary Consul*, like *The Power and the Glory* and *The Heart of the Matter*, seeks to penetrate beneath our encrusted orthodoxy to show that the redeeming quality of human love is one of the evidences of "the appalling strangeness of the mercy of God."

*   *   *

No widely read writer in America writes so fully from the Christian world-view as does John Updike. A Lutheran by up-bringing and now a Congregationalist, he experienced a religious training which he has described as "branding me with a Cross." His mature belief has been influenced by his reading of a variety of Christian thinkers—Søren Kierkegaard, Hilaire Belloc, G. K. Chesterton, C. S. Lewis, and the theologians Paul Tillich and Karl Barth. To Barth and his theology Updike has attributed the sustaining of faith during a difficult period.

Updike's own theology, as it appears through his fiction, poetry, and essays, seems to be composed of historic orthodoxy tempered by an awareness of the existential present. Any such blending of history with immediacy forces the artist to find a common denominator in life by which to measure experience. For Updike that common denominator becomes family relations—marriage, parenthood, conflict between generations, the crises of union and disunion within the family. Because Updike possesses an imagination formed from the wellspring of Christian myth, the primary source for his imagery will be the family of Adam. Sometimes the correlation is oblique; often it's not, as in "Outing: A Family Anecdote," where he talks about the town of Pennington, New Jersey, the ancestral hometown.

> All Updikes of my father's generation had a special feeling about the town of Pennington: it was the family Paradise out of whose inheritance they had been cheated. Cain and Abel and Seth, as boys, must have had a similar feeling about Eden. Adam and Eve were in this case the many sons and daughters of Samuel Updike, the Creator.

The individual family is the human race in microcosm. No wonder, then, that many of Updike's major novels and stories— *Rabbit, Run, Of the Farm, Couples, Rabbit Redux,* stories in *The Same Door,* in *The Music School,* and in *Pigeon Feathers*— focus upon the deterioration of trust between husband and wife, the spreading cancer of infidelity among persons in and out of the home. These are mythic amplifications upon the original theme of Eve's defection and Adam's complicity, with all their sorry consequences.

Although he can be faulted for his insistence upon lurid descriptions of sexual acts or the use of sordid language, Updike's purpose remains unimpeachable: it is to show the world in a lapsed condition. The Fall has left unmistakable scars, although intimations of innocence and bliss remain in the sweetness of children and in recollections of early married days. Modern man tries, of course, by indirection and euphemism to cover matters over. Yet the fact of the Fall remains indelible, an embarrassment to psychoanalysts and their patients alike. Updike's parody of presidential memoirs, "Mr. Ex-Resident," suggests how Adam might have accommodated to the truth's unpleasantness, had he been writing today. Speaking of his family's reaction to life outside Eden, Adam says,

> In my opinion, . . . [Eve] did a wonderful job raising Cain and Abel in an environment that was necessarily unsettled and far from ideal. If the boys did not turn out exactly the way we had hoped, this is no excuse for the disproportionate publicity that has surrounded their quarrel. It is of course a tribute to the office of First Man that everything that happens within his family circle attracts widespread comment.

In spite of modern man's effort to deny or dilute his heritage, the legacy of sin continues to manifest itself in the children of Adam. So in Updike's fiction children all too soon begin demonstrating selfishness and other traits familiar to their parents; likewise first love between husband and wife pales. The story "Should Wizard Hit Mommy?" ends with the young father-husband feeling "caught in an ugly middle position" between his toddler daughter and wife, "and though he as well felt his wife's presence in the cage with him, he did not want to speak with her, work with her, touch her, anything."

This need for withdrawal into privacy, even from those most deeply loved, corresponds to the hiding of Adam and Eve from each other and from God. In modern life the need fulfills itself through prolonged silence, absorption in a solitary task, or as in the case of Harry Angstrom in *Rabbit, Run,* through running away from marriage and its responsibilities.

"Rabbit" Angstrom is the failed hero—the high school basketball star who never made good after the final buzzer ended his last game. Married to Janice, he has no education beyond high school and military service, no concrete ambitions; he holds a succession of mindless jobs. His marriage is corrupted by strife among his in-laws, each set of parents blaming the other family for the young couple's unhappiness. Only a pick-up basketball game in an alley, with teenagers who have never heard of Rabbit Angstrom, can make him feel "liberated from long gloom."

In the first glimpse of Angstrom's domestic life, Updike shows Rabbit and Janice sitting in front of the television set, watching "The Mickey Mouse Club." Jimmy, the adult Mouseketeer, has some advice to offer the audience:

> Know Thyself, a wise old Greek once said. Know Thyself. Now what does this mean, boys and girls? It means, be what you are . . . be yourself. God doesn't want a tree to be a waterfall, or a flower to be a stone. God gives to each one of us a special talent. . . . So: Know Thyself. Learn to understand your talents, and then work to develop them. That's the way to be happy.

The unexpected reference to God in their living room jars Rabbit and his wife because, Updike declares, "both are Christians. God's name makes them feel guilty." But these Christians have allowed their faith, like their marriage, to grow cold; it has all but been abandoned. Neither has any current relationship with the church—Rabbit's family has been Lutheran, Janice's Episcopalian. Rabbit tries to attribute insincerity to Jimmy. Yet, something in the mixture of evangelism with Free Enterprise, Yankee ingenuity, and Greek philosophy stirs an inarticulate response in Rabbit. He is unhappy, the reader infers, because he hasn't developed his God-given talents. Trapped in a dead marriage, he never will.

Later that evening, Rabbit runs for the first time, leaving Janice and driving off into the night, heading south into a vortex of shame and recrimination. After he reaches West Virginia, however, his sense of futility turns him around. But upon arriving back in his hometown, he doesn't return to his wife and child. He runs again, this time to his former coach—for every athlete a father-figure of authority. The dissolute old man, instead of restoring Rabbit to his wife, introduces him to Ruth, a local prostitute, with whom Rabbit lives until Janice is about to deliver their second child. Rabbit then runs from the prostitute back to his wife. But Janice, who is now drinking heavily, accidentally drowns the infant while bathing her.

At the burial ceremony Rabbit runs once more, figuratively, when he retreats behind blaming Janice, blurting out to the grieving families, "Don't look at me. I didn't kill her. . . . She's the one." Then literally he runs from the cemetery, and soon "he feels the wind on his ears even before, his heels hitting heavily on the pavement at first but with an effortless gathering out of a kind of sweet panic growing lighter and quicker and quieter, he runs. Ah: runs. Runs."

Rabbit Angstrom runs from responsibility, from those who need him, from those who would remind him of his own prayer earlier in the novel, "Help me, Christ. Forgive me. Take me down the way." He may think that he's running toward a new beginning, as at the outset of his abortive escape by automobile he kept studying a map of Pennsylvania and seeing Paradise, near Lancaster. "His eyes kept going back to this dainty lettering on the map. He had an impulse . . . to drive there." But now in his soul he knows his route will end in "a huge vacant field of cinders."

"The abdication of belief," says Emily Dickinson, "makes the behavior small." Rabbit Angstrom, having run from God and home, has shrivelled into a smallness that frightens him. He feels an emptiness, a vastness, as "his heart goes hollow." He is, he thinks, "infinitely small and impossible to capture." But Updike, like Francis Thompson, knows better.

> I fled Him, down the nights and down the days;
> I fled Him, down the arches of the years;
> I fled Him, down the labyrinthine ways
> Of my own mind . . .

but all in vain. For the God from whom man runs is also the very Ground on which he runs. The important point, expressed in this novel by the Episcopal priest Eccles, is that a man must keep his heart open for God's grace. Because that grace is limitless and, as the old hymn says, "greater than all our sin," it pursues even the fleetest runner—the Hound of Heaven chasing the Rabbit.

In a belated sequel, *Rabbit Redux*, Updike shows how far and through how many hazards the pursuit may lead. Ten years have passed, the Angstroms have reestablished their shaky marriage. But now, just while Neil Armstrong is taking his giant step for mankind, Rabbit learns that Janice is carrying on an affair. The symbols are appropriate in their contrast of hero and cuckold, the athleticism of an astronaut and the collapsed stamina of the ex-athlete. The reader infers the wife's retribution upon a faithless husband by taking for her lover a used-car salesman, the living token of deceit in American life.

The word *redux* means "returned to health after disease," but the recovery Updike offers is circuitous and mined with danger. Rabbit has become a superpatriot, a Vietnam hawk, a bigot. Through a series of encounters—with a runaway hippy girl who becomes his lover, with a black Jesus named Skeeter—Harry Angstrom finds his categories smashed. Hatred isn't love, sex isn't joy; riots in a black ghetto are no different from the violence in suburban Penn Villas, where his white neighbors set fire to his house.

At Janice's urging they meet after the fire. She has ended her affair, she wants peace. Harry makes the peace sign with his fingers, then ironically holds them to his head, the cuckold's horns. Janice doesn't see the connection, Rabbit's acknowledgment of humiliation as a means of restoring peace. Having no home of their own, they are reunited at the Safe Haven Motel.

There has been no kneeling at the altar rail, no penitence expressed in theological terms. The reconciliation is halting, both verbally and physically, which explains why Updike

chooses to end his novel with an ambiguous question mark.
Together in bed in a strange motel room, we see them: "He.
She. Sleeps. O. K.?" The rhetoric characterizes their separate-
ness; the question mark leaves many difficulties in their relationship unresolved. But here Updike grasps a religious truth known
to the devout—known to the writer of the Song of Songs, to
the Apostle Paul, to Augustine, Dante, and John Donne, then
somehow lost to most Christians since the rise of Victorian
prudery: the truth that conjugal love and sexual ecstasy are the
primary metaphors to describe the love of Christ for his Church.
If there is to be any reconciliation, any act of grace mediating
between husband and wife, it will result in a physical expression
of love or else remain incomplete.

Updike isn't saying that two people who have hurt each other
can solve all their problems by jumping into bed with each
other. That would be the religion of *eros,* the gratification of
self over others. Christianity is the religion of *agape,* the
redeeming love of God poured out for all mankind. Therefore,
if Harry and Janice Angstrom are to know any peace together,
there must be some asking of forgiveness, some offering of hope.
This happens when Harry tells Janice, "I feel so guilty." "About
what?" she asks. "About everything." "Relax. Not everything is
your fault." "I can't accept that," he says, but at least the first
few struggling words have been spoken.

The novels *Of the Farm* and *Couples* demonstrate by negative
example what happens to the spirit when men and women
exchange the glory of sexual love sacramentalized in marriage
for the grossness of mere eroticism.

The narrator in *Of the Farm,* Joey Robinson, has recently
divorced his wife of twelve years, yielding over his three children, to marry a divorcee. With her and her son he visits his
mother on the homestead farm. Joey had met his bride with his
first wife at a party and knew immediately that she could be
taken. Their affair had begun soon after, leaping prematurely
from desire to need. From this new woman Joey had obtained
what he felt to be freedom, "and this freedom," he says, "once
tasted, lightly, illicitly, became as indispensable as oxygen to me,
the fuel of a pull more serious than that of gravity."

Under his mother's harsh scrutiny, Joey now knows his
mistake. He has put his life out of joint. When his mother
declares flatly, "You've taken a vulgar woman to be your wife,"

he agrees: "It was true." On Sunday morning in the Lutheran
church with his mother (his wife and son don't attend church),
he hears a sermon from Genesis 2, the creation of Woman. As
Melville provided Father Mapple's sermon on Jonah as a key
to understanding *Moby-Dick*, so Updike offers the text of this
Lutheran pastor's sermon. The sermon deals with the dignity of
labor, the significance of language, and most importantly to
this novel, the relationship of wife to husband, of women to men.

The pointedness of the text isn't obscured by the young
preacher's "rotundly enunciated and quaintly learned" exposi-
tion. Joey knows the depth of meaning in the words from Genesis: "This is now bone of my bones, and flesh of my flesh." At
the sermon's end, he shakes the minister's hand but avoids
looking him in the eye. Joey Robinson is another of Updike's
backslidden Christians who have forgotten God. He believes; he
feels convicted "of unworthiness, of guilt, of the world being a
colorful final parade that I had somehow missed." But he leaves
the farm and his mother to return with his wife to New York,
his escape made necessary because he can't bear further con-
frontation with truth.

"It's hard to move without touching other lives," Joey Robinson had told his mother. The disruption of a marriage, like a
stone tossed into a placid pond, sends out its waves in concentric
circles. *Of the Farm* reveals the shock of divorce upon the
immediate four persons in the narrative and only suggests the
anguish of several others. *Couples* expands the drama to include
ten families who, according to one member of the clique, have
"made a church of each other"—a religion of *eros*. Sex in all its
libidinous distortions occupies the minds and bodies of these
suburban adults. They have become obsessed with lust, they
exist for no other purpose than to fornicate with another's
partner. As the title of another Updike story states, their lives
have been blighted by Eros Rampant.

But two members of the group, the principal lovers in the
novel, are also genuine church members. Here as before, Updike
holds before his reader an objective standard, the faith and
practice of New Testament Christianity, claimed by his characters as the governing principle of their lives. Now it becomes the
origin of their gnawing consciences. The man, Piet Hanema,
may be taken as Updike's representative Christian, fallen into
a morass of concupiscence. "God help me," he prays, "help me,

get me out of this." But as his carnality tightens its grip upon him, Piet experiences spiritual despair, a dark night of the soul with nightmares of every form of violent death imaginable. Like Claudius in *Hamlet*, he seeks consolation in prayer.

> Horribly awake, Piet tried to pray. His up-pouring thoughts touched nothing. An onyx dust of gas above his face. Something once solid had been atomized. *Thou shalt not covet. Whosoever lusteth in his heart.* . . . Forgive me. Reach down and touch. He had patronized his faith and lost it. God will not be used.

Piet Hanema is a modern-day Lot, as Updike himself says in the novel. He has left a faith nurtured by the Dutch Reformed church for the tepid doctrines of Congregationalism. He has pitched his tents near Sodom and become in the eyes of his companions a cause for further mockery of God and the Church. Of course, the church in suburban Tarbox isn't free from blame. When Piet attends, he finds only "the desiccated forms of Christianity" instead of the powerful Word of God. "How blithe was God, how carefree: this unexpected implication encouraged Piet to live"—but not to repent! So when the fire of God falls on Tarbox, as it does in the form of lightning, it consumes the Congregational church, and Updike adds his condemnation: "The old church proved not only badly gutted but structurally unsound: a miracle it had not collapsed of itself a decade ago."

Updike holds that a church without power has no reason to exist. It is a sham, an abomination before God. Such churches are filled with men like Piet Hanema and Credo, in Updike's story "Believers," who while reading Augustine's *Confessions* finds it impossible to continue: "He cannot go on, he has waited four decades to read this, his heart cannot withstand it. It is too strict and searing, fierce and judicious; nothing alloyed can survive within it."

John Updike demands the unalloyed commitment, beginning with the fundamental premise that "in the beginning God created." This is the starting point, he affirms; for "if the first article of the Creed stands," he says in a personal essay, "the rest flows as water downhill."

> That God, at a remote place and time, took upon Himself the form of a Syrian carpenter and walked the earth willfully healing and abusing and affirming and grieving, appeared to me quite in the character of the Author of the grass.

This same logical flow, from the given proposition of a Creator to the divine absurdities of truth, leads a young boy in the story "Pigeon Feathers" to see his place in the providential order and to see the reality of the resurrection. The boy David asks his pastor, during catechism class, to explain what the Creed means by "the resurrection of the body." The minister falters, caught by his own unbelief, looking for some way to wiggle out of the net of his public recitation of insincerity. His best effort is to explain Heaven and the resurrection as "the goodness Abraham Lincoln did lives after him." But David isn't fooled; nor is he put off by his mother's evasions. He has memorized the passage in John 14:6, "I am the way, the truth, and the *life*," and, Updike tells us, "he would not be wooed from the truth."

He finds the truth about Life Everlasting in a demonstration from nature. He has been asked to shoot some bothersome pigeons and, having done so, prepares to bury them.

> He dug the hole, in a spot where there were no strawberry plants, before he studied the pigeons. He had never seen a bird this close before. The feathers were more wonderful than dog's hair, for each filament was shaped within the shape of the feather, and the feathers in turn were trimmed to fit a pattern that flowed without error across the bird's body. . . . As he fitted the last two, still pliant, on the top, and stood up, crusty coverings were lifted from him, and with a feminine, slipping sensation along his nerves that seemed to give the air hands, he was robed in this certainty: that the God who had lavished such craft upon these worthless birds would not destroy His whole Creation by refusing to let David live forever.

We hear, of course, the echo from two thousand years ago:

> Are not two sparrows sold for a penny? And not one of them will fall to the ground without your Father's will. But even the hairs of your head are all numbered. Fear not, therefore; you are of more value than many sparrows (Matthew 10:29-31, RSV).

To be "robed in certainty" is the believer's privilege. Updike finds, to his dismay, that much of American Christianity prefers equivocation, shuns the imperatives of doctrine, and then wonders at its symptoms of structural decay. John Updike is an artist, not an evangelist. His method is usually indirect, often paradoxical. But his poem "Seven Stanzas at Easter" offers a straightforward challenge to professing Christians, a call to bold faith unadulterated by compromise.

> Make no mistake: if He rose at all
> it was as His body;

if the cells' dissolution did not reverse, the molecules
    reknit, the amino acids rekindle,
the Church will fall.

. . . .

Let us not mock God with metaphor,
analogy, sidestepping, transcendence;
making of the event a parable, a sign painted in the
    faded credulity of earlier ages:
let us walk through the door.

. . . .

Let us not seek to make it less monstrous,
for our own convenience, our own sense of beauty,
lest, awakened in one unthinkable hour, we are
    embarrassed by the miracle,
and crushed by remonstrance.

CHAPTER SEVEN

in my end is my beginning

Some men's conversion to Christian faith reaches far beyond reckoning. Consider Saul of Tarsus, Augustine of Hippo, Thomas Becket of Canterbury, Dwight L. Moody of Northfield, or William A. Sunday of Ames, Iowa. While we are told that God is no respecter of persons, still we find it easy to suppose that there may be greater rejoicing over the Shepherd's finding a lost prince or politician than a lost poet. After all, the potential witness of a mere writer of verses can scarcely be compared to the influence of a Christian statesman! Perhaps for that reason we hear of so few prayer breakfasts along Publishers' Row.

Yet when the record of this century is complete, one of its most dramatic moments, so far as Christian witness is concerned, will have been the quiet announcement in 1927 that Thomas Stearns Eliot—author of "The Love-Song of J. Alfred Prufrock," "Gerontion," *The Waste Land*, and "The Hollow Men"—had affirmed his faith and joined the Church.

In the realm of letters it might be said of T. S. Eliot, more than of any other writer in this century, "Why, man, he doth bestride the narrow world / Like a Colossus." For to Eliot had been given the uniquely double gift of being both a great artist and a powerful arbiter: he was both poet-dramatist and critic. For fully fifty years he led the English-speaking world into fresh discoveries of the potential for its own language. Most importantly, he did so during the last four decades of his life as a confessing Christian believer. His plays and criticism—both literary and social—touched the nerve of Anglo-American civilization; but it is primarily as a poet that Eliot is known, and his poetry is the subject of this chapter.

* * *

Eliot came to his belief out of a childhood and early adult-

hood spent in diluted Unitarianism and, later, skepticism. Born
in St. Louis, Missouri, in 1888, the scion of transplanted New
England aristocrats, college presidents, and preachers, Eliot
bound himself to the tradition of his forebears. He dedicated
himself to the life of the mind, studying at Harvard, the
Sorbonne, and Oxford; writing a doctoral dissertation on the
philosophy of F. H. Bradley; making sporadic attempts at writing experimental verse patterned after French Symbolist poets.
Throughout these years, to the midpoint of his life, he sophisti-
catedly rejected in Christian orthodoxy its gospel of personal
redemption.

The result, as all the world knows, was a vision of life as a
subexistence, the journey of man "through certain half-deserted
streets," across a parched and weary land, and into the Valley
of Death. Those making this journey were, in the poet's opinion,
as good as dead already; in fact, he sometimes spoke of them
with reference to characters found at various stages of torment
in Dante's Hell. They were to become familiar by name as
models of modern Western decadence.

First, there was J. Alfred Prufrock, a timid, indecisive denizen
of genteel society—balding, atrophied, middle-aged, sexually
impotent, self-deluded as to his former accomplishments, frustrated by inadequacy, and "in short, . . . afraid." From the
epigraph to the poem, taken from Canto 27 of The Inferno, the
reader supposes that Prufrock, like Guido da Montrefeltro, has
chosen to be starkly honest with his audience, confident that
what he says can never be repeated to his shame. We meet this
man, therefore, stripped of costume and pose, willing for once
in his life to tell the truth about himself.

The truth he tells cannot be summarized in question and
answer form. Indeed, the question itself is too large, too over-
whelming, to bear being asked. Instead the truth must be
comprehended through observation and experience. "Let us go
and make our visit," he suggests, and the reader follows Prufrock
through the city to his haunts: high teas, social receptions, rooms
where "the women come and go / Talking of Michelangelo,"
coffee klatches, cocktail hours, and assignations. At each and
all of these parties, however, Prufrock confesses that he is
uneasy, disoriented by the whirl of life around him, and wholly
incapable of making a personal relationship.

Prufrock's discomfort stems from lack of confidence in himself

and an awareness that life is rapidly passing him by. The yellow
fog may take its time to settle; all of nature may indulge itself
in "time yet for a hundred indecisions, / And for a hundred
visions and revisions." But for Prufrock the moment is immi-
nent; the moment calls for action, action of which Prufrock is
incapable. His inertia, however, cloaks itself in the pretense
that he too has *time,* time to forestall even further the action
he dare not take for fear that he will "disturb the universe."
To his confidant-auditor Prufrock admits the terror that prevents
him from reaching out for human contact. In its place, he must
settle for the depersonalization of casual encounters, the vacu-
ousness and insincerity of "a formulated phrase," the ennui of a
life "measured out . . . with coffee spoons."

His failure is most poignant when he attempts a sexual liaison.
Lacking both the inclination and the presumptive energy "to
force the moment to its crisis," he nonetheless wishes to sustain
the impression as the debonair man of the world. But his
witty remarks fall flat, his mysterious allusion to Lazarus goes
unnoticed, and his coy mistress is as bored by the whole charade
as is Prufrock himself.

The truth about life's futility becomes clear when Prufrock
despairingly, if rhetorically, asks,

> And would it have been worth it, after all,
> Would it have been worth while,
> . . . .
> After the novels, after the teacups, after the skirts
>   that trail along the floor—
> And this, and so much more?

The answer, of course, is *No* in thunder! None of life's pleasures
can be considered worth the effort. But beyond that, Prufrock
finds himself unable to express himself: "It is impossible to say
just what I mean!" he cries. He is hindered by the fact that he
is not Prince Hamlet, the dramatic nonpareil of eloquence;
instead, he is a bumbling Polonius,

> Full of high sentence, but a bit obtuse;
> At times, indeed, almost ridiculous—
> Almost, at times, the Fool.

The candor of Prufrock's self-scrutiny has had an eroding
effect on his already collapsing image of himself. He has aged,
so much that he fears to wear swimclothes; so much that he
hopes to disguise his baldness with a new hairstyle; so much

that he fears to test his dentures on a peach. Each of these fears testifies to a damaged ego, but Prufrock the erstwhile libertine now undergoes the maximum rebuff: rejection by the mermaids. As figures of sexual fantasy, the sirens of the sea have frequently been employed in literature and in contemporary advertising to suggest the ultimate orgiastic experience. Prufrock has all this in mind when he declares, "I do not think that they will sing to me."

Through the mediating powers of confession, quite independent of religious penance, Eliot brings the persona called Prufrock to a startling awareness of his condition. He is essentially a dead man, drowned as he admits in a maelstrom of license and debauchery. To paraphrase Eliot is a crime, but the meaning of Prufrock's concluding three lines may be this: We have immersed ourselves in grossest sensuality, both real and fantastic, attended by erotic pleasures, until (like Walter Mitty, wakened from his daydreams of power by the reality around him) we come to consciousness and discover that we have indeed been overwhelmed.

The "Love-Song" concludes in resignation to the fact that J. Alfred Prufrock (or T. Stearns Eliot, as the poet called himself in his earliest ascriptions) has lost the central purpose for living: to give meaning to his own existence. In the end, the meaning he seems to give fails to satisfy, so that he would say of his life—as others have said to him—

> "That is not it at all,
> That is not what I meant, at all."

The same sorry report seems to issue from the speakers in all of Eliot's early poems—"Portrait of a Lady," "Rhapsody on a Windy Night," "Aunt Helen," after whose death the household servants no longer need to be discreet about their sexual encounters. The need to bring fulfillment and peace out of the chaos of modern life marks all these urban and urbane poems. But the best emotion of which Eliot's personas are capable is a sentimental fancy, at the end of "Preludes,"

> The notion of some infinitely gentle
> Infinitely suffering thing.

Yet lest the reader be left with the false impression that the speaker, whose previous description of city life has included "the thousand sordid images / Of which your soul was constituted," is about to wallow in sentimentality, he quickly retorts,

> Wipe your hand across your mouth, and laugh:
> The worlds revolve like ancient women
> Gathering fuel in vacant lots.

This is the vision of life offered by the young Eliot, expatriated from America and settled in London as a bank clerk working below the street level. Could it be that his employment, the drudgery of his sums and the meanness of his quarters, failed to lift his vision? Or was the world indeed populated with the likes of Sweeney, Burbank, Bleistein, Doris, and of course Prufrock? The testimony of the Old Man, the speaker in "Gerontion," points to this latter opinion.

"Gerontion" is the despairing cry of a confessed sensualist who now, in old age, has lost his physical senses, his passion, and has only his terror of the inevitable future to sustain him. The poem speaks from the curious vantage of Belief-in-Disbelief; that is, the Old Man *believes* he is condemned and condemned because of his *disbelief*. "After such knowledge, what forgiveness?" he asks. In his youth he had received the sign given for all men's redemption, the Incarnation of the Liberating Word, "the word within a word"; but it was a sign rejected. With its rejection went the knowledge of forgiveness, its place taken by tears, the fruit of Eden's "wrath-bearing tree."

It is important to remember that this poem was written in 1919, still several years before Eliot's public confession of faith. It cannot be doubted, however, that Eliot was moving toward faith, and this contention is well supported by a careful reading of subsequent major poems, *The Waste Land* and "The Hollow Men."

But if Eliot was being impelled toward a commitment in faith as early as "Gerontion" seems to indicate, one reason for his hesitancy before making his decision may have been the very nature of the Church itself. He would not have been the first prospective convert to be dismayed by the Church's failings. In "The Hippopotamus" Eliot amusedly caricatures "the True Church" in contrast to the outcast hippopotamus, a type of the natural man whose relationship with God exceeds even that of the Established Church.

The poem begins, as do so many of Eliot's, with an epigraph whose meaning enlarges the total effect of the poem. It is a quotation, in Latin, from a letter of Saint Ignatius to the Christians at Tralles, written around 100 A.D. A translation would read:

> Likewise let all people reverence both the Deacons, as commanded by Jesus Christ; and the Bishop, as Jesus Christ, the living Son of the Father; the Elders, however, as the council of God and the union of the Apostles. Without these it is not called a church; I am exhorting you about these things as I believe.

A second epigraph quotes Colossians 4:16 (KJV):

> And when this epistle is read among you, cause that it be read also in the church of the Laodiceans.

The reader who knows the New Testament finds his first clue to what Eliot may have intended in the Pauline reference to "the church of the Laodiceans." For while St. Paul appears to have held the Laodicean church in as high regard as the Colossian ("For I want you to know how strenuous are my exertions for you and the Laodiceans," Colossians 2:1), the more familiar reference to the Laodiceans is the much less complimentary description in Revelation 3:14-16:

> To the angel of the church at Laodicea write: "These are the words of the Amen, the faithful and true witness, the prime source of all God's creation: I know all your ways; you are neither hot nor cold. How I wish you were either hot or cold! But because you are luke-warm, neither hot nor cold, I will spit you out of my mouth.

"The Hippopotamus" reverberates with biblical and ecclesiastical allusions: "flesh and blood," "based upon a rock," "God works in a mysterious way," "Blood of the Lamb" are some of the more obvious. The ugly hippo stands throughout the poem in direct contrast to "the True Church." But though "the True Church can never fail," though the Church enjoys material wealth (as did also the Laodiceans), though the Church claims to be "one with God," it is the hippopotamus and not the Church that finds eventual union with God. The picture that Eliot flashes upon the screen of our imagination is unforgettable, the more so, perhaps, because of its apparent absurdity! Imagine, a hippopotamus "performing on a harp of gold"! Yet this is what Eliot declares:

> He shall be washed as white as snow,
> By all the martyr'd virgins kist,
> While the True Church remains below
> Wrapt in the old miasmal mist.

"The True Church" is the church at Laodicea—"the most

pitiful wretch, poor, blind, and naked" (Revelation 3:17). Poor in the midst of great financial resources; blind in spite of the city's fame as a center for the healing of eye diseases; naked in spite of an active and fashionable clothing industry: this was the Laodicean church as the Risen Christ condemned it. The reason for its failure was not hard to find. Having shut out the Lord of the Church, so that he must knock for readmission (Revelation 3:20), the Laodiceans had lost their religious distinctive, the whetstone that gave a cutting edge to their evangelical witness. The Laodiceans were now marked by compromise and complacency; they were successful and popular in the community precisely because they were no longer committed to the unpopular truth of the Gospel. They had lost conviction in what they claimed to believe. They were, at best, lukewarm, fit only to be spat out in disgust!

This too was the Christian Church as Eliot saw it at age thirty. In another poem, "Mr. Eliot's Sunday Morning Service," the poet offers the same kind of contrast, between the ordained presbyters of the Church and Sweeney, Eliot's favorite example of the common man. Origen and other theologians and ecclesiastics make the doctrine of the Word difficult to understand: What does it mean that "the Baptized God" became man in the flesh? Eliot offers an ironic suggestion in the person of Sweeney, who sits, not within the stained-glassed cathedral, but in his tub!

> Sweeney shifts from ham to ham
> Stirring the water in his bath.

Once again the picture is absurdly comic—that a low-life man such as Sweeney might bear a greater resemblance to the Incarnate Word than does "enervate Origen"! Yet it is a truth to be reasserted again and again in Eliot's poetry of belief, as in these lines from the ninth chorus in "The Rock":

> The LORD who created must wish us to create
> And employ our creation again in His service
> Which is already His service in creating.
> For Man is joined spirit and body,
> And therefore must serve as spirit and body.
> Visible and invisible, two worlds meet in Man;
> Visible and invisible must meet in His Temple;
> You must not deny the body.

But before Eliot would be able to declare that the body is the

temple of the Holy Ghost, he must first cross the ragged borders
of the Waste Land. The poem, published in 1922, demands a
fuller study than can be given here, but even at a glance the
reader can perceive the progression that is occurring in Eliot's
religious sensibility. Images of aridity and sterility blend with
allusions to the Sinai desert and to Ezekiel's valley of dry bones.
Spliced among these metaphors are dramatic vignettes, dialogues suggesting the later Eliot's verse-dramas, revealing the
desolation within the soul of modern man and pointing to the
necessity of death before there can be life.

According to Eliot's own commentary on *The Waste Land*,
the principal narrator is Tiresias, "the most important personage
in the poem, uniting all the rest." Eliot goes on, "What Tiresias
sees, in fact, is the substance of the poem." Tiresias, of course,
is the blind prophet of Thebes who first confronts Oedipus with
his guilt. In the *Odyssey* he retains his prophetic powers, even
in the Underworld, where Odysseus consults him. Throughout
literature, wherever the figure of Tiresias appears, his physical
blindness stands in contrast to the greater spiritual blindness of
those to whom he witnesses of the truth. Literary tradition,
therefore, encourages us to take seriously—indeed, to *believe*—
that what Tiresias says is true.

Everywhere Tiresias looks with his inner and unblinded eyes,
he sees death. The title of the first section prepares the reader
for the theme of the poem: "The Burial of the Dead." Even
though the month is April and the season spring, still the world
is full of death and dying: "broken images," "the dead tree,"
"the dry stone," "fear in a handful of dust." Fear also emanates
from a handful of cards, the Tarot cards of Madame Sosostris:
"One must be so careful these days," she warns a fortune-seeking
customer. Everywhere the quotation from *Tristan und Isolde*
applies, "Desolate and empty the Sea." When Tiresias views
the London crowd on its way to work, he exclaims,

> I had not thought death had undone so many.
> Sighs, short and infrequent, were exhaled,
> And each man fixed his eyes before his feet.

Section two, "A Game of Chess," depicts a lavishly appointed
room, complete with all the elements of luxury—rich jewels,
rich furnishings, rich aromas. But above the "antique mantel"
hangs a painting of Philomela, whose tongue was cut out by the
villain Tereus; the remaining walls of the room are also framed

by works of art portraying "other withered stumps of time."
Eliot's picture clearly shows mankind in ruined condition, even
surrounded by the best life has to offer. Mankind has been
checkmated by Time and Death. The only alternative left is to
wait for the end, overcoming despair by immersion in the
foolish fads of a postwar hilarity—in this case, the jazz rhythms
of a popular dance, suggested by Eliot's verses:

> But
> O O O O that Shakespeherian Rag—
> It's so elegant
> So intelligent

And, one might add, so fleeting in its satisfaction! The dancer is
left with too much time and too little profitable to accomplish:

> "What shall I do now? What shall I do?"
> "I shall rush out as I am, and walk down the street
> "With my hair down, so. What shall we do to-morrow?
> "What shall we ever do?"

The aimlessness reminds us of two contemporaneous Americans,
Daisy Buchanan and Jordan Baker in F. Scott Fitzgerald's *The
Great Gatsby*. Nick Carraway remembers Daisy's saying,

> "Do you always watch for the longest day of
> the year and then miss it? I always watch for the
> longest day in the year and then miss it."
> "We ought to plan something," yawned Miss
> Baker, sitting down at the table as if she were
> getting into bed.
> "All right," said Daisy. "What'll we plan?" She
> turned to me helplessly: "What do people plan?"

But frustration and ennui belong to all classes—not merely to
English aristocrats and American *nouveaux riches* but to all
human pawns. So in the pub scene that concludes the second
part of the poem, the dialogue corroborates Tiresias's observation that "we are in rats' alley / Where the dead men lost their
bones." Time, mutability, decay, and the destruction of human
life blend with the warning cry of the pub owner at closing
hour, "HURRY UP PLEASE ITS TIME." The inferences here
are clear: Time has run out, the final reckoning is at hand.
The mind floods with contradictory impressions. On the one
hand, we hear a favorite parting song, "Goodnight, ladies . . .
Merrily we roll along," while on the other, we are reminded
of mad Ophelia's plaintive farewell.

The poet's slight suggestion of Hamlet's rejected lover serves as a bridge between the second and third parts of the poem. For "The Fire Sermon," section three, inveighs by example against the fire of lust, showing as before that concupiscence is emblematic of spiritual death. Eliot has said as much already in his allusion to the Philomela legend, in which all the principals lose their lives because of Tereus's rapacity. And in the pub scene just concluded, one of the conversations overheard by Tiresias centers around Lil's attempted abortion, after she had nearly died with her fifth child. "You are a proper fool," the Cockney gossip declares.

> Well, if Albert won't leave you alone, there it is, I said,
> What you get married for if you don't want children?

Having already recalled *The Great Gatsby* and the similarity in attitudes there, I am reminded of Gatsby's freeloading guest Klipspringer and his parody of a popular song for the age, "Ain't We Got Fun?"

> One thing's clear and nothing's clearer:
> The rich get rich and the poor get — children!

Sex—meaningless, joyless, mechanical sex—burns through "The Fire Sermon," revealing again that all ranks of persons, from the queen and her courtiers to the humble typist, may be cut down in its holocaust. Curiously, or so it seems at first, much of the imagery of this section is drawn from London's River Thames. But the river in this poem is more properly the river of fire that flows through Hades. London has become Carthage, a city renowned for its wickedness, as St. Augustine tells us in his *Confessions*. As this section comes to its close, Eliot introduces a rhetorical device to show that man's mere consciousness of peril is insufficient to effect his salvation: the exhausted, gasping prayer that line by line grows weaker. It is a device we shall see used again.

> Burning burning burning burning
> O Lord Thou pluckest me out
> O Lord Thou pluckest
> burning

But the prayer is ineffectual; the end is death, whether by burning—or by drowning, the fate of Prufrock, the fate predicted by Madame Sosostris: "Fear death by water."

In section four, "Death by Water," Eliot needs only eight lines to sketch his scenario and to comment on its awful consequences. The Phoenician merchant Phlebas, dead for a fort-night, has long since forgotten "the profit and loss" that marked the degrees of his success or failure in life. Sucked down into the vortex of death's reality, the merchant can no longer distinguish one stage of life from another. All has been erased.

This, of course, is plain enough from the text. What is also plain yet highly unusual is Eliot's warning to the reader:

> Gentile or Jew
> O you who turn the wheel and look to windward,
> Consider Phlebas, who was once handsome and tall as you.

Eliot has been so urbane, so sophisticated to this point; yet here he is, calling out a doomsday prophecy like a revivalist. But there is no salvation offered in Eliot's call. He is merely alerting the unwary voyager, offering counsel against the inevitable dis-aster awaiting every man who ventures forth upon the sea. The warning is stated in terms appropriate to the preoccupation in this poem with appearance, physical beauty, sexuality, and the vigor of life. Phlebas had all of these in a body "handsome and tall." Yet now he is dead.

But perhaps Phlebas is the fortunate one, for at least his death seems to have brought to cessation the agony of existence. Not so for those who remain, the living dead condemned to suffer Death-in-Life. One of these sufferers speaks through most of the final section, "What the Thunder Said." His fate is to wait for death "with a little patience"; his situation remains the barren wilderness of "rock and no water and the sandy road." His circumstances are clearly desperate, even when compre-hended only at the level of poetic description.

But Eliot here is doing more than merely describing a general scene of deprivation. He is also trying to enter into the experi-ence of those whose last hope for survival was a religious hope and who have seen that hope destroyed by crucifixion. For, remarkably, Eliot the skeptic is portraying the despair of dis-belief through the dramatic persona of an unnamed witness to the death of Jesus.

We have a clue to this speaker's identity: he may be the anonymous companion of Cleopas (Luke 24:13-35), who with him encountered the Risen Lord on the Emmaus road. If this is so, then certainly Eliot has taken license with Luke's record—that both Cleopas and the other recognized the Lord in the

breaking of bread and hurried to tell the good news of the resurrection. For purely dramatic reasons it is enough that the
speaker in "What the Thunder Said" has no such good news.
For him all that can be said about Jesus may be summed up
in one line:

> He who was living is now dead.

He remembers the arrest of Jesus in Gethsemane, the divine
refusal to speak before false accusers, the torture-chamber tech-
niques of Roman justice, all as a crescendo of violence:

> The shouting and the crying
> Prison and palace and reverberation
> Of thunder of spring over distant mountains.

He remembers the Place of the Skull as "Dead mountain mouth
of carious teeth that cannot spit." He remembers even the
onlookers along the Via Dolorosa. But most of all he remembers
and remembers and remembers the thirst—unquenchable for
the dying, unquenchable for the living.

> If there were water
> And no rock
> If there were rock
> And also water
> And water
> A spring
> A pool among the rock
> If there were the sound of water only
> Not the cicada
> And dry grass singing
> But the sound of water over a rock
> Where the hermit-thrush sings in the pine trees
> Drip drop drip drop drop drop drop
> But there is no water

Throughout *The Waste Land* there has been ample suggestion
of water: rain, rivers, the sea, its tides and currents; all these
flow and flood. But these are not the waters to quench man's
thirst; these are not the Water of Life. They are cruel, surprising rains, polluted rivers, seas of desolation and destruction.
They bring no refreshing, no relief. They are "empty cisterns
and exhausted wells."

This same hopelessness of tone carries on to the speaker's
experience in the Emmaus road passage. His inability to account
for the mysterious Third Party becomes a lament: "But who is
that on the other side of you?" Uncertain of New Life, he

must turn instead to visions of climactic disorder and catastrophe—a barbarian assault by "hooded hordes" upon the centers of Western civilization, from Jerusalem to London; the inversion and collapse of meaning; the final denial of purpose, to the accompaniment of Peter's crowing cock. The opportunity for redemption is forever gone; only judgment follows.

Eliot's note on this section declares one of his intentions to be a representation of "the present decay of eastern Europe." He refers presumably, in 1922, to the 1917 Bolshevist revolution and its subsequent terrors. But the judgment to be dispensed is not political but personal; its canons are neither Christian nor Marxist but Hindu; it comes not from priest or worker but from the voice of the thunder, speaking only three words. These words, translated as "Give," "Sympathize," and "Control," are to be interpreted as questions: "What have we given?" To these questions only the most faltering responses may be made, for when the truth is told, man has not given of himself; he has not offered sympathy; he has not bound himself to self-control.

The Waste Land concludes in resignation and acceptance of the inevitable. London Bridge is indeed falling down; what, then, does it matter whether or not one leaves his affairs in order? The only defense remaining, the speaker tells us, lies in "these fragments . . . shored against my ruins." Fragments of memory and desire, lines of songs, allusions dredged from a mythic unconscious, and the desperate, mad determination to fight it through to the end—these only can provide the "Shantih" or peace in an absurd condition whose only salvation is doom.

"The Hollow Men," written in 1925, brought readers one degree nearer to the brink of damnation, to the beach of Acheron, the river that flows through Dante's Hell. There we find a special class of wretched souls—the uncommitted, the no-accounts who take no stand. Their tolerance has exhausted them; they are mere scarecrows. In their elliptical description of themselves,

> Shape without form, shade without colour,
> Paralysed force, gesture without motion. . .

the omission of both subject and verb suggests a lack of identity and an incapacity for action.

The Hollow Men are dead, but only in the same manner of

speaking by which we have already recognized Prufrock, Gerontion, and various speakers in *The Waste Land* as "dead." That is, they are spiritually dead; they have not yet "crossed / With direct eyes to death's other Kingdom." They fear such a transition, for it will mark an irreversible commitment, involuntary yet irrevocable.

At the same time, however, the Hollow Men cling to one final shred of hope. This is the hope that through passage into "death's twilight kingdom" they might fall under the grace of "the perpetual star," perhaps the same grace described by Graham Greene as "the appalling strangeness of the mercy of God." This, Eliot writes, is

The hope only
Of empty men.

Otherwise they are abandoned in the cactus land, condemned to the treadmill existence, reciting their litany against the backdrop of failure to love, to create, to believe. As in "The Fire Sermon," the human voice at prayer fades as the reality of the world's impending doom breaks through:

This is the way the world ends
Not with a bang but a whimper.

The Hollow Men capitulate, submitting to their fate with only the slightest token of protest.

This poem marks the nadir of man's experience in Eliot's poetry. Beyond the depths of the Hollow Men's descent lies an unknown gorge whose depths Eliot never plumbed because he was himself beginning his upward spiritual climb. It should now be clear that for Eliot the climb was an undertaking commenced long before his public statement of belief; at what exact point it began, perhaps no one can say. We have the recorded statement that, in 1927, on a visit to Rome, Eliot surprised his travelling companions by falling to his knees in St. Peter's basilica.

It does not require much imagination, however, to find Eliot's own testimony in his first poem published after his expression of faith, "Journey of the Magi," issued as a Christmas greeting in the same year. The narrator of this poem, an aged Magus, is dictating his memoirs to an amanuensis. He recalls details of the strange journey made so long ago in quest of the King. It was, he recalls, "a cold coming" and "a hard time." Hardships of the season, hostility and unreliability among men, even the

lameness of the camels: all these are remembered. But added
to these woes, and greater than them all, were

> the voices singing in our ears, saying
> That this was all folly.

When Eliot draws his narrator on to remember their eventual
arrival at the house where the Child could be found, the poet
begins introducing concrete references to the New Testament—
references which must be seen as transcending the experience
of the Wise Man himself. He saw only an infant; he never knew
the significance of "three trees on the low sky," "vine-leaves
over the lintel," the gamblers "dicing for pieces of silver," or
"the empty wine-skins." Yet to the reader who knows the story
of Redemption, there can be no mistaking the weight of these
allusions to the Cross, the Passover signs of blood and wine, and
all the rest of Eliot's rich texture of imagery.

The Magus, like Eliot himself, is undramatic about the climactic moment of his journey. Addressing his secretary, old
man instructs, "It was (you may say) satisfactory." But if the
meeting with God-in-Flesh is related in a restrained tone of
understatement, it only serves the more to heighten the experience and questioning that follow. For the act of worship—what
Matthew describes as homage and the presentation of lavish
gifts (Matthew 2:11)—has consequences that pursue the Wise
Men for the rest of their lives.

> All this was a long time ago, I remember,
> And I would do it again, but set down
> This set down
> This: were we led all that for
> Birth or Death? There was a Birth, certainly,
> We had evidence and no doubt. I had seen birth and death,
> But had thought they were different; this Birth was
> Hard and bitter agony for us, like Death, our death.
> We returned to our places, these Kingdoms,
> But no longer at ease here, in the old dispensation,
> With an alien people clutching their gods.
> I should be glad of another death.

The fervor with which Eliot writes in this stanza leaves no
doubt as to his conviction. The urgency with which the aged
Magus insists that his question be answered leaves no doubt
as to its importance. The answer, of course, is to eliminate the
choice between Birth and Death and to see them joined together
in a theological truth. The Incarnation was begun in birth and

fulfilled in the sacrificial death at Calvary. But the Wise Man's experience was of an opposite order: it began in "hard and bitter agony" that led to the death of the old ways, "the old dispensation," so that New Life could be born. Forever after, the Magus would be a stranger in his own kingdom, so much so that he willingly looks for "another death," a physical death that transports him to a new Kingdom.

Eliot's poetry had always been religious; that is, it had always treated of that which some theologians call "ultimate concern." So Eliot's confession of faith did not transform him suddenly into a "religious poet." In fact, he quite rejected most religious poetry as "pious insincerity," adding that "people who write devotional verse are usually writing as they *want* to feel, rather than as they do feel." What Eliot became was a Christian poet—a poet whose world-view had been radically altered because he had turned from the ways of Death to the Way of Life. He had found a place to stand, penetrating by faith to "the still point of the turning world."

There Eliot saw a new vision of life beyond the Waste Land, a new perception of meaning beyond the daily dance around the Prickly Pear. It was a vision of supreme transcendence, based he said upon "the belief, for instance, in holy living and holy dying, in sanctity, chastity, humility, austerity."

The poetry Eliot wrote thereafter reflects his arrival in a safe harbor after a stormy voyage. It has been criticized by some readers—George Orwell and Alfred Kazin, for example—as having lost that very quality of fear and speculation that gave his early work its throbbing reality. "Eliot was better," Kazin once told me, "before he found all the answers." There is a sense in which I would agree; purely as drama, Prufrock's anxieties make far more interesting reading than does the discovery in "Ash-Wednesday" that believers may find "our peace in His will." Yet it was the quietude of profound faith that enabled Eliot to write, as his valedictory, the *Four Quartets*, contemplative in mood yet unmistakable in power.

Nor can one resist noting that during the same period of Eliot's search for a central point of focus, an end in his beginning, the older Irish poet William Butler Yeats was declaring the onset of chaos in "The Second Coming." For Yeats, whose syncretist attempts at molding a satisfying creed out of pagan ritual and religious quackery left him without hope, there could be no motionless center, no integrated wholeness to life. In 1927, while Eliot was beginning a new relationship with life and all of nature through a new relationship with God, Yeats was asking in despair,

> O chestnut-tree, great-rooted blossomer,
> Are you the leaf, the blossom, or the bole?
> O body swayed to music, O brightening glance,
> How can we know the dancer from the dance?

T. S. Eliot had accepted as true the paradox proclaimed by Jesus Christ, that one must lose his life in order to find it, that death-to-self is the only means of knowing a rebirth into everlasting life. He said all this quite straightforwardly in "East Coker," one of the great *Four Quartets*.

> You say I am repeating
> Something I have said before. I shall say it again.
> Shall I say it again? In order to arrive there,
> To arrive where you are, to get from where you are not,
> You must go by a way wherein there is no ecstasy.

And in the next section of the poem:

> Our only health is the disease
> If we obey the dying nurse
> Whose constant care is not to please
> But to remind of our, and Adam's curse,
> And that, to be restored, our sickness must grow worse.

But Eliot's conversion to Christianity, which so markedly changed his view of life and literally put a new song in his mouth, did not escape the scoffer's notice. That same year, an issue of *The Exile*, a literary magazine edited by Eliot's former mentor Ezra Pond, carried the following contribution:

> *NEO-THOMIST POEM
> The Lord is my shepherd, I shall not
> want him for long.
>
> *The title 'Neo-Thomist Poem' refers to
> temporary embracing of church by
> literary gents—E.H.

"E. H." were the initials of Ernest Hemingway, whose cynicism could not permit Eliot the possibility of a genuine confession of faith. Eliot had come to know what Hemingway could admit only at the business end of a shotgun—that life is more than bravado and the ephemeral satisfaction that comes from living by the world's code. Again in "East Coker" he said it plainly,

> Not the intense moment
> Isolated, with no before and after,
> But a lifetime burning in every moment.

Beyond the sophistication of Prufrock, the desperado gaiety of the Waste Landers, and the surreal terror of the Hollow Men, Eliot had found something of ultimate importance. The early Prufrock and Phlebas the Phoenician had both feared death by water; but now, his peace made with God, Eliot could face the final voyage—no matter how far it carried him out of sight of land—to his soul's fulfillment and the commencement of life everlasting.

> We must be still and still moving
> Into another intensity
> For a further union, a deeper communion
> Through the dark cold and the empty desolation,
> The wave cry, the wind cry, the vast waters
> Of the petrel and the porpoise. In my end is my beginning.

*   *   *

Any writer who is Christian accepts the awesome obligation of making known the mystery of God's good news, of proclaiming that Christ is the Liberating Word. Here the Christian writer differs from writers who disbelieve, for while most sane men can see that mankind as a whole lies imprisoned by shackles greater than himself, few know where to look for liberation. Northrop Frye reminds us that Homer wrote, "The gods alone are free," but this is not the Christian view. Man too can be free, as Charles Wesley wrote in 1739:

> He breaks the power of reigning sin,
> He sets the prisoner free.

God's provision for emancipation, as given in the Bible, is quite simple. Jesus Christ is the Incarnate Word, the living expression of Truth. To know him is to know Truth in its ultimate revelation; to know Truth is to be free. "You shall know the truth," Jesus declared, "and the truth will set you free" (John 8:33). To give this promise added emphasis, he continued: "If then the Son sets you free, you will indeed be free" (John 8:36).

But if the Word is to be proclaimed in all its liberating power, then Christ must speak from the pages of novels and stories, poems and plays, with unquestionable clarity. In his ecstasy of praise, the psalmist said, "My tongue is the pen of a ready writer" (Psalm 45:1, KJV). "O Lord," wrote John Updike, "bless these poor paragraphs that would do in their vile ignorance your work of resurrection."

The writer consecrated to such a mission risks the contumely of a rejecting world. The truth he tells differs from the world's accepted falsehoods. "The loneliness of doing right is one of the mysteries of a Christian life"—so wrote the poet Marianne Moore just before her death. The writer and any other Christian must be willing to endure this loneliness. He must be willing, if necessary, to go with John Bunyan to Bedford Jail; to endure with Alan Paton the persecution of an inhumane government; to sacrifice with Boris Pasternak and Aleksandr Solzhenitsyn the Nobel Prize; to persevere, again with Solzhenitsyn, in raising his voice against godless oppression and religious compromise, even at the cost of banishment.

But he must also be willing to speak out boldly in spite of subtler evils—the flattery of popular acceptance, smothering prosperity, or patronizing fame. He must never allow his view of the world to blur. That view from the Cross is a panorama of disaster, as has been said. But because of the Empty Tomb, that view is also the central panel in a triptych of grace, showing the splendor that was Creation and the splendor of Paradise to come.